Balancing Work and New Parenthood

Balancing Work and New Parenthood

A Comparative Analysis of Parental Leave in Australia, Canada, Germany and Sweden

Zarah Denese Ramoso and Guzyal Hill

ANTHEM PRESS

Anthem Press
An imprint of Wimbledon Publishing Company
www.anthempress.com

This edition first published in UK and USA 2023
by ANTHEM PRESS
75–76 Blackfriars Road, London SE1 8HA, UK
or PO Box 9779, London SW19 7ZG, UK
and
244 Madison Ave #116, New York, NY 10016, USA

British Library Cataloguing-in-Publication Data
A catalogue record for this book is available from the British Library.

Library of Congress Cataloging-in-Publication Data
A catalog record for this book has been requested.
2023934784

ISBN-13: 978-1-83998-927-8
ISBN-10: 1-83998-927-0

Cover design by: Zarah Denese Ramoso

This title is also available as an e-book.

CONTENTS

FOREWORD

By Emma Walsh, CEO, Parents at Work and Founder,
Family Friendly Workplaces

'Balancing Work and New Parenthood: A Comparative Analysis
of Parental Leave in Australia, Canada, Germany and Sweden'
(the Monograph)

The approach to paid parental leave (PPL) policy design and rollout
in Australia has been complex and slow when compared internationally.
Australia was one of the last OECD nations to adopt a government-funded
national scheme in 2011 and it remains one of the least generous in terms of
both the length and the amount of paid leave. After more than a decade of
inaction to modernise and adequately fund PPL, Australia's scheme has not
kept pace and now lags significantly behind the majority of other OECD
nations. Consequently, the impact is felt across our economy and society.

Australia's progress on women's economic participation and opportunity
is regressing, according to the World Economic Forum. We have a very
gendered division of labour by international standards. Australia's current
parental leave provisions are no longer considered adequate or fit for purpose.

This insightful paper brings to the fore an extensive exploration of the
'untold story' of Australia's parental leave history and its impacts. The paper
matches historical movements with specific laws highlighting the intricacies
of how Australia compares and contrasts between Canada, Germany and
Sweden and why reform is needed.

It provides a solid baseline from which policymakers can apply international
research and evidence to design a competitive, world-class PPL scheme
for Australia into the next decade. At whilst there is a renewed appetite
by the current federal government to further invest in paid parental leave
and childcare with new policies coming into effect by 2024, fundamentally,
this paper begs the question, will it be enough?

This paper asks: 'who cares about the next generation?', a crucial question that both government and business must confront and rise to meet in a post-Covid economy – the act of care-giving and role of caregivers in our society has never been more exposed as under-valued and under-invested in.

The beneficiaries of well-funded, accessible, gender-equal PPL are not only women and children, in terms of improved health and economic security. It also facilitates greater workforce inclusion and normalises men's ability to contribute to caregiving responsibilities, strengthening family relationships and driving greater economic output. The evidence is clear, PPL is good for families, businesses and our overall economic growth.

With the business case for action being increasingly understood by organisations, there continues to be a rise of progressive employer-funded PPL policies, fuelling the need for the government scheme to keep pace.

PPL inclusions vary significantly between employers. Gender-neutral PPL policies that enable greater opportunity for both parents to flexibly share caring responsibilities are becoming more normalised with the removal of 'primary' and 'secondary' carer labels contributing to a greater take up by men. For example, following the introduction of a shared parental leave policy by one of Australia's 'Big Four' accounting firms in mid 2021, their employee engagement survey found that parents scored 12% above the firm's average when asked whether they planned to stay with the firm for five or more years.

It takes a village to raise a child and that includes Government and business community cooperation – from standards setting and policy development to law amendments. PPL reform needs fast-taking to drive substantial social and economic impact and return on investment for future generations to come, and to make Australia a leading family-friendly a nation.

Chapter 1

INTRODUCTION

I Introduction

A Background

All member countries of the Organisation for Economic Co-operation and Development (OECD), including Australia, guarantee some form of paid parental leave to new parents.[1] These policies differ substantially in the duration of leave provided, amount of benefits, job protection and eligibility.[2] This monograph critically examines paid parental leave in Australia compared with the global framework and the position within select similar OECD member countries. The substantial disparity in parental leave policies between Australia and these OECD member countries raises questions about the effect of Australian policies on gender inequality in the workforce, women's workforce participation and child and parental health. The support of new parents is particularly important in Australia as a country facing the problem of the aging population.

A recent survey in Australia reported that three out of four women returning from work following parental leave spend at least four months at home with their child.[3] Parental leave policies serve as a mechanism for providing new parents, especially women, a leave of absence from work. These leave policies aid new parents in preparing for childbirth, recovering from childbirth and adapting to caring for their child. The goal of these policies is to assist parents to balance competing financial and family responsibilities without having to resign one or the other. Professor Brough and her team established in a seminal

---

1 With an exception of the USA.

2 The Organisation for Economic Co-operation and Development (OECD), *Parental Leave Systems* (PF No 2.1, OECD, August 2019) <http://www.oecd.org/els/soc/PF2_1_Parental_leave_systems.pdf>.

3 Australian Bureau of Statistics, *Pregnancy and Employment Transitions, Australia, November 2017* (No Catalogue No 4913.0, 29 June 2018) <https://www.abs.gov.au/ausstats/abs@.nsf/mf/4913.0>.

qualitative research interviewing 81 parents in Australia and New Zealand that current employment transition is perceived as 'premature and as having adverse personal consequences (e.g., personal health, child attachment and breast-feeding) and organisational consequences (e.g., diminished job commitment and increased turnover intentions).'[4] Additional research demonstrated synergy in perceived organisational support and 'dynamic processes of self-efficacy to regulate work and life in facilitating work–family enrichment'.[5] Which means that working parents who are allowed sufficient time for parenting can also be happy and productive employees.

This monograph recognises that parental leave is available to a number of carers; however, the Australian Bureau of Statistics identified that '95% of all primary carers leave is taken by mothers.'[6] For this reason, the focus of this monograph is on mothers. As a rule, the adoptive parents have the same entitlements as biological parents, therefore the discussion of parental leave entitlements will progress without making a distinction between adoptive and biological parents.[7]

Because of the extensive nature of this topic, this research focused on analysing the effects of parental leave on new mothers and children and was based on feminist theory. The participation of fathers on the arrival of a newborn is equally important; however, the vast majority of primary carers in Australia are mothers, and the effects of the current legal landscape on paternity leave and the men's labour market are beyond the scope of this essay. Although this monograph focuses on women as the majority (95%) of carers,

---

4 Paula Brough, Michael P. O'Driscoll and Amanda Biggs, 'Parental Leave and Work-family Balance among Employed Parents Following Childbirth: An Exploratory Investigation in Australia and New Zealand' (2009) 4(1) *Kōtuitui: New Zealand Journal of Social Sciences Online* 71 ('Parental Leave and Work–family Balance among Employed Parents Following Childbirth').

5 Xi Wen Chan et al., 'Examining the Mediating Role of Self-Efficacy in the Relationship between Perceived Organizational Support and Work–Family Enrichment' (2022) 29 *International Journal of Stress Management* 281; Xi Wen Chan et al., 'Work–Family Enrichment and Satisfaction: The Mediating Role of Self-Efficacy and Work–Life Balance' (2016) 27(15) *The International Journal of Human Resource Management* 1755 ('Work–Family Enrichment and Satisfaction').

6 Australian Bureau of Statistics, *Media Release – One in 20 Dads Take Primary Parental Leave (Media Release)* (Gender Indicators, Australia, September 2017 No 4125.0, 19 September 2017) <https://www.abs.gov.au/ausstats/abs@.nsf/Lookup/by%20 Subject/4125.0~Sep%202017~Media%20Release~One%20in%2020%20dads%20 take%20primary%20parental%20leave%20(Media%20Release)~11>.

7 Fair Work Ombudsman, 'Maternity & Parental Leave', *Fair Work Ombudsman* <https:// www.fairwork.gov.au/leave/maternity-and-parental-leave>.

future research must consider the rights and entitlements of the remaining 5% of the carers to obtain the full picture and better consider the challenges faced by fathers and adoptive carers in Australia.

This monograph commences by identifying different forms of feminist jurisprudence applicable to analysing paid parental leave laws. International legal frameworks are then examined, identifying the sources of law underpinning the right to paid parental leave. Next, the universal Australian parental leave scheme is examined, including paid and unpaid statutory leave, their history and development, employer-provided leave and Australian laws relating to parental leave. Thereafter, three OECD member countries that are economically comparable to Australia (namely Canada, Germany and Sweden) are investigated regarding their paid parental leave provisions. Following the collection of all comparative data, the monograph discusses key elements of the Australian paid parental leave scheme compared with the equivalent schemes in other OECD member countries. The main argument of this monograph is that Australian paid parental leave laws are long overdue for reform. An alternative model is recommended based on the comparisons made. The research conclusions lead to recommendations for Australia to amend its paid parental leave provisions to be on par with other OECD countries.

II Methodology

The analysis of the global framework for parental leave was based on the doctrinal and comparative research methods. The Council of Law Deans described the doctrinal method as a 'rigorous analysis and creative synthesis, the making of connections between seemingly disparate doctrinal strands, and the challenge of extracting general principles from an inchoate mass of primary materials'.[8] The doctrinal method initiates interpretation and qualitative analysis to construct legal doctrines through an examination of the law.[9] It involves reading and analysing primary sources of law, including legislation and case law, together with secondary materials such as journal articles and reports to ascertain what the law is and how the law applies to a particular issue.[10]

---

8 Council of Australian Law Deans, 'Statement on the Nature of Legal Research', *The CALD Standards for Australian Schools* (May 2005) 3 <https://cald.asn.au/wp-content/uploads/2017/11/cald-statement-on-the-nature-of-legal-research-20051.pdf>.
9 Paul Chynoweth, 'Legal Research in the Built Environment: A Methodological Framework' [2008] *Salford University Review* 12.
10 Anthony Bradney, 'Law as a Parasitic Discipline' (1998) 25(1) *Journal of Law and Society* 71.

In this monograph, the doctrinal method was used to examine international conventions and paid parental leave legislation in Australia and the corresponding legislation for the featured OECD member countries. Since Australia's paid parental leave scheme is embedded in legislation, an analysis of the *Paid Parental Leave Act 2010* (Cth), the related legislation and international human rights conventions was conducted. Secondary sources included commission inquiries and reports, which provided a deeper understanding of why paid parental leave provisions were introduced in these countries.

Once the primary sources of law had been established and a review of the secondary sources had been conducted, a comparison of legal provisions within the featured OECD member countries was made using a comparative method. This method considers the comparative aspects of law in the broader international jurisdiction, examining the similarities and differences between the laws of different jurisdictions. The method utilises a combination of doctrinal, theoretical and reform-oriented methods but is categorised under a different area of research because of its different focus.[11] It investigates how similar legal jurisdictions address a common issue,[12] enabling the researcher to critically analyse the law and understand how laws have progressed over time. The method assists in identifying reform options and their respective merits and limitations.[13] For this research, the legislation review and comparison combined with the literature review were used to create reform-oriented research to help drive policy changes where necessary.

---

11 Ibid.
12 Natalia Hanley et al., 'Improving the Law Reform Process: Opportunities for Empirical Qualitative Research?' (2016) 9(4) *Australian & New Zealand Journal of Criminology* 546.
13 Ibid.

Chapter 2

RIGHTS TO PARENTAL LEAVE

A Feminist Jurisprudence

Feminist Jurisprudence, more commonly known as feminism, originated in 1978[1] and comprises a competing and, at times, contradicting collection of social theories, political movements and moral philosophies. Feminism is attributed mainly to women's experiences, particularly with respect to women's social, political and economic inequalities. Advocates of feminist jurisprudence were unable to concur on the most effective way of achieving the end goal of equality for women.[2] Traditionally, advocates promoted either liberalism, based on the concept of 'sameness', or culturalism, based on the concept of 'differences'.[3] While both liberal and cultural feminism have valid grounds, the main argument of this monograph is based on reconstructive feminism because it promotes gender equality by recognising that women as parents have dual familial and societal roles and makes necessary adjustments to empower women in their venture to succeed in both. In addition, reconstructive feminism considers changes in women's roles as mothers through the lenses of shared responsibility with fathers, therefore, parents' entitlements have to be considered as a whole in any future policy development.

1 Liberal Feminism

Liberal feminism—among other varieties of feminism—provides the strongest authority and foundation for other feminist theories. By definition, liberal feminism is a 'feminist theory that believes gender inequality is created

---

1 Patricia A Cain, 'Feminist Jurisprudence: Grounding the Theories' (1988) 4(2) *Berkeley Women's Law Journal* 191, 193.
2 Jennifer E Karr, 'Where's My Dad: A Feminist Approach to Incentivized Paternity Leave' (2017) 28(2) *Hastings Women's Law Journal* 221, 232 ('Where's My Dad').
3 Beth Bernstein, 'Difference, Dominance, Differences: Feminist Theory, Equality, and the Law' (1990) 5 *Berkeley Women's Law Journal* 214, 218.

by lowering access for women and girls to civil rights and allocation of social resources such as education and employment'.[4] The main principle is that individuals should have the right to life, liberty and pursuit of happiness and that no one should bar those rights.[5] The roots of liberal feminism were acquired from the liberal political philosophy in the enlightenment period, and the movement focuses on autonomy, universal rights, equal citizenship, and democracy.[6] Liberal feminists are essentially concerned with deconstructing structural obstructions, including discriminatory laws, which keep women in oppressive gender roles and hinder them from actively participating in the workplace and society.[7]

Liberal feminism can be classified into two categories, namely assimilationist and androgynous. The assimilationist paragon assumes that all people have equal status and should consequently be treated according to the same rules and principles.[8] In addition to forcing women to abide by the rules created by men, the assimilationist ideal ignores the core elements of women's identities by declaring men's behaviour and lifestyle as the standard.[9] The androgynous ideal seeks to eradicate gender differences, pushing for change in men and women's gender roles and behaviour to create a society without gender differences.[10] Generally, liberal feminism assumes that the differences between men and women are not biological, which at its core represents reproduction differences.[11] This assumption can be problematic because liberal feminism cannot overcome the underlying

---

4 Bimer Eyayu Enyew and Alemeneh Getaneh Mihrete, 'Liberal Feminism: Assessing Its Compatibility and Applicability in Ethiopia Context' (2018) 10(6) *International Journal of Sociology and Anthropology* 59, 60 ('Liberal Feminism').

5 Ibid.

6 Rosemarie Tong, *Feminist Thought: A More Comprehensive Introduction* (West View Press, University of North Carolina, 4th ed, 2013) <http://site.ebrary.com/id/10819756>.

7 Joan Scott, 'Deconstructing Equality-versus-Difference: Or the Uses of Poststructuralist Theory for Feminism' in Diana Meyers (ed), *Feminist Social Thought* (Routledge, 1997) 758 <https://philmonographs.org/rec/MEYFST>.

8 Iris Marion Young, *Justice and the Politics of Difference* (Princeton University Press, 1990).

9 Tong (n 19); Christine Littleton, 'Reconstructing Sexual Equality' in Diana Meyers (ed), *Feminist Social Thought* (Routledge, 1997) 715 <https://philmonographs.org/rec/MEYFST>; Young (n 19).

10 Ibid.

11 Margaret W Sallee, 'A Feminist Perspective on Parental Leave Policies' (2008) 32(4) *Innovative Higher Education* 181, 185.

notion that men and women are intrinsically different.[12] However, liberal feminism has successfully demonstrated to a degree that while men and women are different, women are not inferior to men.[13]

2 Cultural Feminism

Contrary to liberal feminism, which ignores women's differences, cultural feminism acknowledges and believes that women's differences from men should be celebrated.[14] Cultural feminism embraces women's differences to make them the epitome of their identities.[15] In this process, cultural feminism aims for underappreciated feminine characteristics to be given merit.[16] These characteristics may include women's ability to give birth to a child and their natural tendency to be more nurturing than men.[17] Thus, cultural feminism argues that instead of disregarding differences, patrons must advocate for policies that consider women's specific needs.[18]

Cultural feminism strongly relies on female biology, namely, that a woman is distinguished by her anatomy.[19] However, differences between men and women are not merely biological[20] since biological differences induce social differences. Specifically, women present feminine characteristics through their biology and society's perception of them as a result of their biology.[21]

Although cultural feminism celebrates these differences, it creates particular difficulties. Cultural feminism has the propensity to assume that all women share the same identity and experiences because they share the same biology.[22]

---

12 Hester Nienaber and Nthabiseng Moraka, 'Feminism in Management Research: A Route to Justly Optimise Talent' (2017) 16(2) *Acta Commercii* 139 <https://www.researchgate.net/publication/312259716_Feminism_in_management_research_A_route_to_justly_optimise_talent>.

13 Ibid.

14 Bernstein (n 16) 218–19.

15 Linda Alcoff, 'Cultural Feminism versus Post-Structuralism: The Identity Crisis in Feminist Theory' (1988) 13(3) *Signs: Journal of Women in Culture and Society* 405.

16 Ibid.

17 Sallee (n 24) 187.

18 Scott (n 20).

19 Alcoff (n 28).

20 Young (n 21); Littleton (n 22).

21 Sallee (n 24) 187.

22 Alcoff (n 28); Nancy Fraser and Linda Nicholson, 'Social Criticism without Philosophy: An Encounter between Feminism and Postmodernism' in Diana Meyers (ed), *Feminist Social Thought* (Routledge, 1997) 132 <https://philmonographs.org/rec/MEYFST>.

As a result, there tends to be a generalisation that the ideal woman is the same across all societies,[23] but that is simply not the case. Cultural feminism also fails to consider women who manifest more traditionally masculine traits and novel feminine aspirations.[24] Notwithstanding the power vested on women by claiming their own identity, it is questionable whether such identity fits women or has been forced to fit by way of centuries of oppression.[25] By relying on womanhood's definition as something originally developed by men, cultural feminism triumphs only in preserving a cycle of sexism and assuming that women bear the onus of childbirth and parenthood.

3 Reconstructive Feminism

The principal theory of reconstructive feminism is that gender differences, real or perceived, build social disadvantage when women are measured against unmentioned and unappreciated masculine standards.[26] The main goal of reconstructive feminism 'is to decouple gender from the key habits and conventions that impoverish many men and women—and brutalize anyone who cannot fit into that comfortable dichotomy; ... to catalyse gender flux'.[27] Reconstructive feminism differs from liberal feminism mainly because it accepts the physical differences between men and women.[28] It differs from cultural feminism by maintaining that differences should be inconsequential.[29] Instead of dwelling on the 'sameness' or 'differences' between men and women, reconstructive feminism questions why differences have any significance at all.[30] Reconstructive feminism redirects the focus from women's bodies to social standards.[31] This type of feminism benefits both men and women by eradicating the social standards that adversely affect both genders.[32] Challenging these standards is vital in pursuing more alternatives for both men and women concerning work and family life.[33]

A social system dominated by male-identified, male-controlled and male-centric standards is more likely to value masculinity and masculine

---

23 Sallee (n 24) 187.
24 Joan Williams, 'Reconstructive Feminism: Changing the Way We Talk About Gender and Work Thirty Years After the PDA' (2009) 21 *Yale Journal of Law & Feminism* 79.
25 Sallee (n 24).
26 Williams (n 37) 100.
27 Ibid 99–100.
28 Sallee (n 24) 233.
29 Ibid.
30 Williams (n 37) 99–100.
31 Ibid 102.
32 Ibid 113.
33 Sallee (n 24) 233.

characteristics over femininity and feminine traits.[34] Hence, when women exhibit traits or desires considered traditionally masculine, for example, contributing to the household financially while raising children, they often find themselves at a disadvantage. Some reports of discrimination and disadvantages experienced by employees accessing "family-friendly" employment policies have emerged, with the perception that an employee accessing parental leave provisions is fundamentally less committed to work.[35] The concept of reconstructive feminism defeats this form of disadvantage by disassociating masculinity and femininity from men and women.[36]

Therefore, this monograph views parental leave through the lens of reconstructive feminism. Reconstructive feminism rebuts the presumption that women's foremost role in society is to raise children and, therefore, a woman's needs as the standard caretaker come before her needs as an alternative provider or a breadwinner. By offering women sufficient duration and amount of paid parental leave, women can also financially provide for their families alongside raising children. Consequently, women will be viewed as equally valid providers within a societal context and transition to initial parenthood financially rewarded by the society (including employers or governments). Reconstructive feminism might be particularly important in situations of single parents or in situations when fathers wish to assume the role of the primary carer.

B Global Frameworks

By adopting three fundamental global human rights instruments, Australia has made a commitment to maternity protection, to preserve the human rights of women and children and to promote gender equality. These instruments are the *Convention on the Elimination of All Forms of Discrimination Against Women*[37] ('CEDAW'), the *International Covenant on Economic, Social and Cultural Rights*[38] ('ICESCR') and the *Convention on the Rights of the Child*[39] ('CRC').

---

34 James Poniewozik, 'Paternity Leave and Why Men Need Feminism Too', *TIME* (online, 10 June 2014) <https://time.com/2853080/fathers-day-gift-paternity-leave-feminism-for-men/>.

35 Paula Brough and Michael P O'Driscoll, 'Organizational Interventions for Balancing Work and Home Demands: An Overview' (2010) 24(3) *Work & Stress* 280 ('Organizational Interventions for Balancing Work and Home Demands').

36 Sallee (n 24).

37 *Convention on the Elimination of All Forms of Discrimination against Women*, opened for signature 18 December 1979, 1249 UNTS 13 (entered into force 03 September 1981) ('CEDAW').

38 *International Covenant on Economic, Social and Cultural Rights*, opened for signature 16 December 1966, 993 UNTS 3 (entered into force 03 January 1976) ('ICESCR').

39 *Convention on the Rights of the Child*, opened for signature 20 November 1989, 1577 UNTS 3 (entered into force 2 September 1990) ('CRC').

1 Convention on the Elimination of All Forms of Discrimination Against Women

Australia became a signatory to the CEDAW in 1979 and ratified it in 1983.[40] The Preamble of the CEDAW foreshadows the requirement of maternity leave with pay or comparable social benefits for mothers. The Preamble provides that 'the social significance of maternity and the role of both parents in the family and in the upbringing of children, and that the role of women in procreation should not be a basis for discrimination but that the upbringing of children requires a sharing of responsibility between men and women and society as a whole.'[41]

Article 11(2)(b) states the obligation of States in relation to paid maternity leave. It provides that:

'In order to prevent discrimination against women on the grounds of marriage or maternity and to ensure their effective right to work, States Parties shall take appropriate measures:
… (b) To introduce maternity leave with pay or with comparable social benefits without loss of former employment, seniority or social allowances…'[42]

Upon ratification of this convention, the Australian Government made a reservation that it is unable to fully implement Article 11(2)(b) in introducing paid maternity leave or with comparable social benefits throughout Australia. Although the Australian Government introduced the *Paid Parental Leave Act*[43] ('the Act') in 2011, the reservation has not been withdrawn. In 1999, the Human Rights and Equal Opportunity Commission recommended that the Australian Government remove its current reservation,[44] however this process has yet to be initiated.

---

40 Australian Government Department of Foreign Affairs and Trade, 'Treaties - Convention on the Elimination of All Forms of Discrimination against Women', *Australian Government Department of Foreign Affairs and Trade* (Web Page, 20 December 2018) <https://www.info.dfat.gov.au/Info/Treaties/treaties.nsf/AllDocIDs/333D22 B9ED69B058CA256B300024F1BA>.

41 CEDAW (n 50) Preamble.

42 Ibid art 11(2)(b).

43 *Paid Parental Leave Act 2010* (Cth).

44 Human Rights and Equal Opportunity Commission, *Pregnant and Productive: It's a Right Not a Privilege to Work While Pregnant* (Report of the National Pregnancy and Work Inquiry, Australian Human Rights Commission, 1999) 229 <https://humanrights. gov.au/our-work/pregnant-and-productive-its-right-not-privilege-work-while-pregnant-1999>.

2 *International Covenant on Economic, Social and Cultural Rights*

Australia became a signatory to the ICESCR in 1972 and ratified it in 1975.[45] Article 10 provides that 'The States Parties to the present Covenant recognize that special protection should be accorded to mothers during a reasonable period before and after childbirth. During such period working mothers should be accorded paid leave or leave with adequate social security benefits.' According to the UN Committee on Economic, Social and Cultural Rights ('UNCESCR'), the obligation imposed by Article 10 is that paid maternity leave must be accorded to women involved in all types of occupation and be given for a sufficient duration.[46]

Article 3 ensures the right of equality between men and women in the enjoyment of economic, social, and cultural rights. The UNCESCR has stated that Article 9 of the Convention which relates to the right to social security, a country must guarantee adequate maternity leave for women, paternity leave for men, and parental leave for both men and women in its implementation of Article 3.[47] Australia, however, has been behind introduction of equal parental leave for both men and women. At the time of writing, there is a considerable disparity between the duration of leave available to mothers and fathers respectively.

3 *Convention on the Rights of the Child*

The CRC was ratified by Australia on 17 December 1990.[48] One of the CRC's core principles is that 'the best interests of the child shall be

---

45 Australian Government Department of Foreign Affairs and Trade, 'Treaties - International Covenant on Economic, Social and Cultural Rights', *Australian Government Department of Foreign Affairs and Trade* (Web Page, 6 February 2009) <https://info.dfat.gov.au/Info/Treaties/treaties.nsf/AllDocIDs/CFB1E23A1297FFE8CA256B4C000C26B4>.

46 UN Committee on Economic, Social and Cultural Rights, *General Comment No. 19: The Right to Social Security (Art. 9 of the Covenant)* (UN Doc E/C. 12/GC/19, 04 February 2008, adopted 23 November 2007) <https://www.refworld.org/docid/47b17b5b39c.html> para 19.

47 UN Economic, Social and Cultural Rights, *General Comment No. 16: The Equal Right of Men and Women to the Enjoyment of All Economic, Social and Cultural Rights (Art. 3 of the Covenant)* (UN Doc E/C. 12/2005/4, 11 August 2005) <https://www.refworld.org/docid/43f3067ae.html>.

48 Australian Government Department of Foreign Affairs and Trade, 'Treaties - Convention on the Rights of the Child', *Australian Government Department of Foreign Affairs and Trade* (Web Page, 14 March 2007) <https://www.info.dfat.gov.au/Info/Treaties/treaties.nsf/AllDocIDs/E123F4F71DCAE3E7CA256B4F007F2905>.

a primary consideration' regarding all actions concerning children.[49] Further, the CRC provides that State Parties shall take 'all appropriate legislative and administrative measures' in ensuring the protection of the bests interests of the child.[50] The CRC also imposes an obligation on State Parties to 'ensure to the maximum extent possible the survival and development of the child.'[51]

The CRC acknowledges that the health and well-being of children are intrinsically dependent on the lives of their parents.[52] The CRC has extensive provisions outlining obligations relevant to the provision of paid maternity leave, the main provision being Article 18 which provides that:

> 'For the purpose of guaranteeing and promoting the rights set forth in the present Convention, States Parties shall render appropriate assistance to parents and legal guardians in the performance of their child-rearing responsibilities and shall ensure the development of institutions, facilities and services for the care of children.'[53]

As a State Party to the CRC, Australia has an obligation to 'take all appropriate measures to ensure that children of working parents have the right to benefit from child-care services and facilities for which they are eligible.'[54] Further, the CRC prescribes that Australia must ensure access to 'basic knowledge of child health and nutrition, [and] the advantages of breastfeeding.'[55]

The Committee on the Rights of the Child indicated some concerns regarding Australia's compliance with its international obligations under the CRC, in particular, articles 18 and 24:

> 'The Committee is concerned that women working in the private sector are not systematically entitled to maternity leave, which could result in different treatment between children of State employees and those

---

49 CRC (n 52) art 3(1).
50 Ibid art 3(2).
51 Ibid art 6(2).
52 Human Rights and Equal Opportunity Commission, Submission No 128 to Productivity Commission, *Inquiry into Paid Maternity, Paternity and Parental Leave* (6 February 2008) para 67.
53 CRC (n 52) art 18(2).
54 Ibid art 18(3).
55 Ibid art 24(2).

working in other sectors. … The Committee encourages the State party to review its legislation and make paid maternity leave mandatory for employers in all sectors, in the light of the principle of the best interests of the child and articles 18 (3) and 24.'[56]

C International Labour Organization Standards

The International Labour Organization ('ILO') is a specialised United Nations agency bringing together governments, employers, and workers from 187 member States (including Australia) to set labour standards, develop policies and devise programs which promote decent work for all men and women.[57] One of the main goals of the ILO is the adoption of international labour standards to aid member countries in the implementation and process through supervision and technical assistance.[58] ILO standards take the form of Conventions or Recommendations which serves as a benchmark for the provision of human rights.[59] The ILO standards provide the legal foundation in the pursuit of a universally decent working conditions, and it is a result of various discussions between governments, workers and employers based on their respective experiences from all the over the world.[60] Therefore, ILO standards on maternity protection are intrinsically pertinent to the development and improvement of national laws and policies in this field.[61]

Over the course of its history, the ILO has adopted three Conventions on maternity protection. These Conventions (together with their corresponding Recommendations) have gradually stretched the scope and entitlements of maternity protection at work.[62] Their central targets are to enable women to successfully combine their reproductive and productive roles, and to eradicate employment discrimination due to their reproductive role.[63]

---

56 International Labour Organization, 'About the ILO', *International Labour Organization* (Web, Page 2021) <https://www.ilo.org/global/about-the-ilo/lang--en/index.htm>.
57 Ibid.
58 International Labour Organization, 'International Rights and Guidance on Maternity Protection at Work' in *Maternity Protection Resource Package: From Aspiration to Reality for All* (International Labour Organization, 2012) 7.
59 Ibid.
60 Ibid.
61 Ibid.
62 Ibid.
63 Ibid.

1 *Maternity Protection Convention, 1919 (No. 3)*

The *Maternity Protection Convention, 1919 (No. 3)*[64] ('C003') was the first ILO standard for the employment of women before and after childbirth. C003 was limited to women working in public or private industrial or commercial undertakings.[65] It describes the basic principles of maternity care: the rights to maternity leave (12 weeks), medical benefits, income replacement during leave and breastfeeding breaks.[66] The right to leave was fortified by the express prohibition of dismissal during a woman's absence on maternity leave or at such time that the notice would expire during such absence.[67] Although C003 is no longer open to ratification, it remains in force for those Member States who have ratified it and have not subsequently denounced it.[68]

2 *Maternity Protection Convention (Revised) (No. 103)*

The *Maternity Protection Convention (Revised) (No. 103)*[69] ('C103') was adopted in 1952 and extended the scope of protection to a remarkably wider category of workers. This includes women employed in industrial undertakings, non-industrial and agricultural occupations which also include 'domestic work for wages in private households.'[70] Moreover, it extended leave entitlements to cover illness arising from pregnancy or confinement and expanded on the types of medical benefits provided.[71] It also inaugurated a minimum level of cash maternity benefits which should be fixed at a rate sufficient for the 'full and healthy maintenance of herself and her child in accordance with a suitable standard of living.'[72] Although C103 is also no longer open to ratification, it remains in force for Member States who have ratified it[73]

---

64 *Maternity Protection Convention, 1919 (No. 3)* (entered into force 13 June 1921).
65 Ibid.
66 Ibid art 3.
67 Ibid art 4.
68 International Labour Organization, 'Ratifications of C003 - Maternity Protection Convention, 1919 (No. 3)', *International Labour Organization* (Web Page, 2017) <https://www.ilo.org/dyn/normlex/en/f?p=NORMLEXPUB:11300:0::NO::P11300_INSTRUMENT_ID:312148>.
69 *Maternity Protection Convention (Revised), 1952 (No. 103)* (entered into force 07 September 1955).
70 Ibid art 1.
71 Ibid art 3.
72 Ibid art 4(2).
73 International Labour Organization, 'Ratifications of C103 - Maternity Protection Convention (Revised), 1952 (No. 103)', *International Labour Organization* (Web Page, 2017) <https://www.ilo.org/dyn/normlex/en/f?p=1000:11300:0::NO:11300:P11300_INSTRUMENT_ID:312248>.

and have neither subsequently denounced it nor have subsequently ratified Convention No. 183 (in which case, only the latter Convention remains in force).

3 Maternity Protection Convention, 2000 (No. 183)

The *Maternity Protection Convention, 2000 (No. 183)*[74] ('C183') replaced both C003 and C103, making it the most up-to-date international labour standard on maternity protection as accompanied by its corresponding *Maternity Protection Recommendation, 2000 (No. 191)*[75] ('R191').

C183 and R191 are notable for various improvements in maternity protection from earlier standards. First, C183 expanded the scope of maternity protection to cover all employed women, including those in 'atypical' forms of dependent work in the informal economy.[76] C183 also increased the minimum leave to 14 weeks,[77] while R191 suggests an 18-week minimum leave provision.[78] Further, C183 provides a more robust employment protection[79] and requires measures to guarantee that maternity does not lead to employment discrimination.[80] For example, C183 expressly prohibits pregnancy tests as part of a candidate selection procedure,[81] except in very limited specific circumstances.

Despite the fact that Australia has not ratified the C183, Conventions are often referred to with authority as the internationally recognized minimum standard.[82] Moreover, the *Australian Constitution*,[83] provides that the external affairs power can be relied on to give legislative effect to ILO standards.[84] Nevertheless, Australia currently offers 18 weeks of paid parental leave, which is consistent with Article 4 of C183 and Article 1 of R191.

---

74 *Maternity Protection Convention, 2000 (No. 183)* (entered into force 07 February 2002).
75 International Labour Organization, 'Maternity Protection Recommendation, 2000 (No. 191)', *International Labour Organization* (Web Page, 2017) <https://www.ilo.org/dyn/normlex/en/f?p=NORMLEXPUB:12100:0::NO::P12100_ILO_CODE:R191>.
76 *Maternity Protection Convention, 2000 (No. 183)* (entered into force 07 February 2002) art 2(1).
77 Ibid art (4).
78 International Labour Organization, 'Maternity Protection Recommendation, 2000 (No. 191)' (n 83) art 1.
79 *Maternity Protection Convention, 2000 (No. 183)* (n 84) art 8.
80 Ibid art 9.
81 Ibid art 9(2).
82 International Labour Organization, 'International Rights and Guidance on Maternity Protection at Work' (n 68) 7.
83 *Australian Constitution* s 51(29).
84 Ibid.

Chapter 3

AUSTRALIA'S PAID PARENTAL LEAVE

A Paid Parental Leave Scheme

Despite public pressure and several attempts by private entities to introduce paid parental leave, it was not introduced in Australia until 2010. Since its introduction, paid parental leave arrangements have been limited, and current arrangements fall significantly below international standards.

1 History of Paid Parental Leave

In 2009, the Productivity Commission was tasked by the Australian Government to undertake a public inquiry regarding paid maternity, paternity and parental leave. At the time of the inquiry, there was a substantial disparity across the Australian workforce regarding access to paid parental leave provisions.[1] Almost one out of two female employees did not have access to paid maternity leave.[2] However, public servants had some form of paid parental leave available to them.[3]

At the conclusion of the inquiry, the Productivity Commission outlined its recommendations in its report entitled: 'Paid Parental Leave: Support for Parents with Newborn Children' ('Report').[4] The main recommendation of the Report was the introduction of a statutory paid parental leave scheme in Australia. Recommendation 2.1 provided that the paid parental leave scheme should be for a total of 18 weeks, which could be shared by eligible parents, with an additional two weeks of paternity leave reserved for the father sharing the same daily primary care of the child; the payments were equivalent

---

1 Australian Government Productivity Commission, *Paid Parental Leave: Support for Parents with Newborn Children* (Inquiry Report No 47, Productivity Commission, 28 February 2009) <https://www.pc.gov.au/inquiries/completed/parental-support/report/parental-support.pdf>.
2 Ibid.
3 Ibid.
4 Ibid.

to the adult federal minimum wage for each eligible week.[5] Recommendation 2.6 provided that all those employed with a reasonable degree of attachment to the labour force should be eligible, including the self-employed, contractors and casual employees.[6] Recommendation 2.7 noted that a broad range of family types should be eligible, including conventional couples, lone parents, non-familial adoptive parents, same-sex couples and non-parental primary carers in exceptional cases, as long as they met the employment test.[7]

The Report outlined that the proposed scheme would meet a range of commonly agreed objectives. First, it would generate maternal and child health and welfare benefits through the projected increase in time off parents could obtain from work.[8] Through this time off, a considerable number of families would have an increased capacity to provide exclusive parental care for children for six to nine months.[9] Second, the scheme would promote essential, publicly supported goals within society, particularly so that having a child and taking time off for family reasons could be viewed by society as part of the ordinary course of work and life for working parents.[10] The scheme would also contribute potentially six months of additional employment for the average woman over her lifetime.[11] Finally, the scheme would increase retention rates for businesses, with decreased training and recruitment costs.[12]

According to the Report, the promotion of child and maternal health is one of the strongest reasons for supporting a statutory paid parental leave scheme.[13] Moreover, the Report recognised that it could be hazardous for women to return to work early.[14] The Report also utilised evidence relating to child and parental wellbeing, revealing that six to nine months is the ideal duration of postnatal absence from work.[15] The 18-week statutory paid parental leave, in addition to an employee's personal leave, would allow parents a recourse of at least 26 weeks without causing serious financial burden.[16]

---

5 Ibid xxxix.
6 Ibid xli.
7 Ibid xiv.
8 Ibid 1.5.
9 Ibid 2.45.
10 Ibid 1.5.
11 Ibid xiv.
12 Ibid.
13 Ibid D12.
14 Ibid D10.
15 Ibid xx.
16 Ibid.

The Report was comprehensive and was the earliest study to assess the effects of paid parental leave in Australia extensively. Recommendation 2.15 of the Report provided that the Australian Government should commission surveys to assess the effects of the government's statutory paid parental leave scheme on parents' behaviours, the existing voluntary schemes and the health and welfare of parents and children.[17] However, it is over 10 years since the release of the Report and the commencement of the *Paid Parental Leave Act 2010* with no further action.

2 *The Paid Parental Leave Act*

The *Paid Parental Leave Act 2010* introduced a paid parental leave scheme for parents who were primary carers of children born or adopted from 1 January 2011 onwards. The Australian Government funded the scheme as a response to the 2009 Productivity Commission Report.[18]

The object of the Act is to financially support primary carers of new babies to allow carers to take time off work to care for the child after childbirth or adoption; enhance maternal and child health and development; encourage women's workforce participation; promote gender equality and work and family life balance.[19] The scheme provides working mothers and the initial primary carers of adopted children with access to up to 18 weeks parental leave pay at the national minimum wage while they stay at home to look after their baby or adopted child.[20] The scheme was designed to complement parents' existing entitlements like employer-provided paid parental leave and all forms of annual leave.[21] Parents can lodge their claims until three months before the expected date of birth or adoption of the child.[22]

The first requirement for claiming paid parental leave under the Act is that the claimant should be the 'primary carer' of a child. A person is a primary carer of a child if the child is in the person's care[23] and that person meets the child's physical needs more than anyone else in such period.[24]

---

17 Ibid xlv.

18 Steve O'Neill et al, 'Paid Parental Leave Bill 2010', *Parliament of Australia* (Bills Digest Service, Parliamentary Library, 15 June 2010) <https://www.aph.gov.au/Parliamentary_Business/Bills_Legislation/bd/bd0910/10bd175#_ftn15>.

19 *Paid Parental Leave Act 2010* (Cth) s 3A.

20 Explanatory Memorandum, Paid Parental Leave Bill 2010 (Cth) 1.

21 Ibid.

22 Ibid.

23 *Paid Parental Leave Act* (n 56) s 47(1)(a).

24 Ibid s 47(1)(b).

For a primary carer to be eligible for paid parental leave, the claimant also needs to meet the work test, income test and residency requirements.[25] First, the primary carer, who in most cases is the mother, must have worked for a total period spanning at least 295 days (10 months)[26] out of the 392 days (13 months) immediately before the expected birth or adoption of a child,[27] without a break greater than eight weeks between any two consecutive workdays.[28] To qualify for the working period, the claimant must have undertaken a minimum of 300 hours of paid work during the 10-month period,[29] which on average is equivalent to one day of work per week.[30] As such, full-time and part-time workers, casual workers, contractors and the self-employed may be eligible for the scheme.[31] Second, the claimant must satisfy the income test prescribed by the Act. A person satisfies the income test if the person's 'adjusted taxable income' in the previous full financial year before the claim or birth (whichever is the earlier) is less than the applicable paid parental leave income limit,[32] which is $150,000.[33] Finally, the claimant will need to be an Australian citizen or permanent resident and, generally, will need to be living in Australia from the date of birth of the child and remain so for the parental leave pay period.[34]

Once eligibility is confirmed, primary carers will receive parental leave pay for up to 18 weeks[35] at the national minimum wage,[36] which is currently $753.80 per week.[37] Most of the time, payment is received by the claimant through their employer,[38] and it is taxable, like salary and wages. In addition to parental leave entitlements for the primary carer, there is a two week payment entitlement for the father or partner. Interestingly, if parents decide that father is going to be the primary carer for the child, mother would not be eligible for

---

25 Ibid s 31(2).
26 Ibid s 32.
27 Ibid s 33.
28 Ibid s 33.
29 Ibid s 32.
30 O'Neill et al (n 115) 2.
31 Explanatory Memorandum, Paid Parental Leave Bill (n 117) 2.
32 *Paid Parental Leave Act* (n 56) s 37.
33 Ibid s 41.
34 Ibid s 45.
35 Ibid s 11(5)(a).
36 Ibid s 65.
37 Australian Government Fair Work Ombudsman, 'Minimum Wages', *Australian Government Fair Work Ombudsman* (Web Page, 2020) <https://www.fairwork.gov.au/>.
38 *Paid Parental Leave Act* (n 56) s 72.

the two-week payment entitlement. As stated on the website of the Services Australia: 'You can't get Dad and Partner Pay if you're the birth mother of the child'.[39] This policy intentionally or unintentionally creates an environment where women who wish to maximise the payments for caring for the children are almost forced to be the primary carers as the entitlements in the opposite scenario would be less. It is unlikely that parents will make the final decision on who is going to be the primary carer on the basis of keeping or losing this entitlement alone, but this inflexibility can become a contributing factor in widening the salary gap between mothers and the rest of Australian society.

3 Amendments to the Paid Parental Leave Scheme

In 2010, the Australian Government introduced the *Paid Parental Leave Act 2010*[40] as a result of the Report's recommendations. The Act provided 'eligible primary carers'[41] with 18 weeks of paid parental leave.[42] The cash benefits while on leave were to be equivalent to the national minimum wage.[43] Subsequently, the World Health Organisation recommended a minimum period of 26 weeks after birth as required for maternal and child health development.[44] By combining the 18-week statutory paid leave and an employee's paid parental leave as part of the worker's employment contract, this internationally recognised standard is met in Australia. However, should an employee be ineligible for paid parental leave from the workplace, 18 weeks is the maximum duration of paid leave the worker can receive, which is well below the 26-week minimum recommendation of the WHO.

In 2013, a proposed amendment on the scheme's duration and generosity was announced. The proposed amendment was directed at extending the length of statutory paid parental leave from 18 weeks to 26 weeks, paid at a rate equivalent to an employee's ordinary earnings instead of the national minimum wage.[45] However, after his opening remarks on Mother's Day

---

39 Australian Government, Services Australia (10 December 2021) <https://www.servicesaustralia.gov.au/who-can-get-dad-and-partner-pay?context=22136>.

40 *Paid Parental Leave Act 2010* (n 56).

41 Ibid s 31(2).

42 Ibid s 7.

43 Ibid s 65(1).

44 World Health Organization, *Global Nutrition Targets 2025: Breastfeeding Policy Brief* (No WHO/NMH/NHD/14.7, World Health Organization, 2014) <http://apps.who.int/iris/bitstream/handle/10665/149022/WHO_NMH_NHD_14.7_eng.pdf?ua=1>.

45 ABC News, 'Promise Check: Provide Mothers with 26 Weeks Paid Parental Leave', *ABC News* (8 May 2016) <https://www.abc.net.au/news/2014-07-27/paid-parental-leave-promise-check/5423690>.

in 2015, the Prime Minister announced that this proposal was to be withdrawn following a review of the 2015 budget, commenting on 'tough times' and 'tight budgets'.[46]

The subsequent proposed amendments to the *Paid Parental Leave Act 2010* came in the Fairer Paid Parental Leave Bill,[47] introduced in 2015. The Bill purported to restrict the availability of the statutory paid parental leave to parents with no employer-provided parental leave or whose employer-provided parental leave was for a period below 18weeks or paid at a rate lower than the national minimum wage.[48] In addition, the Bill nominated to remove the compulsory provision of paid parental leave by employers to eligible employees, except when the employer elected to administer the payment to employees, subject to the consequent approval of the employee.[49]

The Bill was welcomed by the public. By the end of 2016, the Senate Community Affairs Legislation Committee had carriage of a Senate Inquiry and Report concerning the Bill. The Inquiry received a total of 106 submissions, the majority of which expressed strong opposition to the Bill. For example, the Law Institute of Victoria submitted that the Bill would adversely affect women working in the legal profession who become mothers;[50] this would contribute to further disadvantages faced by women in the legal profession.[51] The Queensland Law Society[52] and the Law Council of Australia[53] shared the same views, endorsing the Law Institute of Victoria's submission. In its submission, the Law Council of Australia relied on the results of its study entitled: 'National Attrition and Re-engagement Study (NARS) Report'.[54] The NARS Report examined why women left the legal profession in Australia. It involved collecting and analysing qualitative and quantitative data on women's experiences in the legal profession to identify preliminary

---

46 Tony Abbott, 'Joint Press Conference, Sydney', *Department of the Prime Minister and Cabinet* (Web Page, 5 October 2015) <https://pmtranscripts.pmc.gov.au/release/transcript-24438>.

47 Fairer Paid Parental Leave Bill 2016 (Cth).

48 Parliament of Australia, 'Fairer Paid Parental Leave Bill 2016', *Parliament of Australia* (Web Page, 2017) <https://www.aph.gov.au/Parliamentary_Business/Bills_LEGislation/Bills_Search_Results/Result?bId=r5752>.

49 Ibid.

50 Ibid.

51 Ibid.

52 Queensland Law Society, Submission No 63 to Community Affairs Legislation Committee, *Inquiry into the Fairer Paid Parental Leave Bill 2016* (12 December 2016) 1.

53 Law Council of Australia, Submission No 53 to Community Affairs Legislation Committee, *Inquiry into the Fairer Paid Parental Leave Bill 2016* (16 December 2016).

54 Ibid.

opportunities to redress the high attrition rate of women.[55] The NARS Report found that 25% of women reported having been discriminated against because of family or carer responsibilities.[56] Further, the Top End Women's Legal Service noted that the Bill would make it more difficult for mothers to incorporate the ideal 26-week parental leave recommended by the WHO.[57] The Northern Territory Anti-Discrimination Commission defended the paid parental leave scheme from claims that it was a 'luxury' and a form of 'double dipping'; instead, the commission submitted that the scheme was a vital part of the structural reform needed to secure women's workforce participation.[58] The Australian Human Rights Commission submitted that the Bill was 'retrogressive' because its proposed limitations to the scheme would cause a reduction in current payments for many women who have access to employer-provided parental leave.[59] The commission also submitted that the Bill did not align with Australia's human rights obligations, particularly in provisions of the ICESCR and the CEDAW.[60] Ultimately, the Bill did not proceed, and it was discharged from the Notice Monograph in 2017.

B Employer-Paid Parental Leave

Employers also provide paid parental leave to eligible employees by way of modern awards and enterprise bargaining agreements. A modern award outlines the 'fair and relevant minimum safety net of terms and conditions' of employees, including leave entitlements, based on industry or occupation.[61] An enterprise agreement, otherwise known as an enterprise bargaining agreement, is an agreement between employers and employees that effectively

---

55 Law Council of Australia, *National Report on Attrition and Re-Engagement Study (NARS) Final Report* <https://www.lawcouncil.asn.au/policy-agenda/advancing-the-profession/equal-opportunities-in-the-law/national-report-on-attrition-and-re-engagement>.

56 Law Council of Australia, Submission No 53 to Community Affairs Legislation Committee (n 150).

57 Top End Women's Legal Service, Submission No 26 to Community Affairs Legislation Committee, *Inquiry into the Fairer Paid Parental Leave Bill 2016* (12 December 2016).

58 Northern Territory Anti-Discrimination Commission, Submission No 64 to Community Affairs Legislation Committee, *Inquiry into the Fairer Paid Parental Leave Bill 2016* (12 December 2016).

59 Australian Human Rights Commission, Submission No 104 to Community Affairs Legislation Committee, *Inquiry into the Fairer Paid Parental Leave Bill 2016* (January 2017) 19.

60 Ibid 17.

61 *Fairwork Act 2009* (Cth) s 134.

supersedes the modern award, applicable with terms and conditions of employment not any less than what is offered in a modern award.[62]

The amount of leave and pay entitlements for employees varies between employers and is dependent on the relevant work agreement, contract or policy. Employer-funded paid parental leave does not affect an employee's eligibility for the Australian Government's paid parental leave scheme. Contrarily, the statutory paid parental leave was designed to complement existing employer-paid parental leave.

Until the introduction of paid parental leave in 2011, Australia's paid parental leave policy had been sourced primarily through the linkage of the employment relationship and the industrial relations system.[63] As a result, unions and employers have had substantial participation in developing paid parental leave in Australia.[64] Overall, the paid parental leave became accessible through intermingled mechanisms like federal and state legislation, awards, enterprise agreements and company policies.[65]

1 Parental Leave as Welfare Payments

Before commencing discussions on modern awards and enterprise agreements, it is important to note historical views on parental leave within the government and industrial relations sphere. In 1912, maternity leave allowances were introduced, payable to all women notwithstanding their employment status.[66] These allowances stemmed from the standpoint that parental leave was a welfare concern of the government instead of being an industrial issue.[67] For example, in 2004, the Family Assistance Legislation Amendment (More Help for Families—Increased Payments) Bill[68] was introduced, which provided a maternity payment (previously known as the 'Baby Bonus') of $3,000, payable as a lump sum to all mothers, regardless of income, from 1 July 2004. The maternity payment progressively increased to $4,000 in July

---

62 Ibid s 172.
63 Marian Baird, 'Parental Leave in Australia: The Role of the Industrial Relations System Work, Family and the Law' (2005) 23(1) *Law in Context: A Socio-Legal Journal* 45, 46.
64 Ibid.
65 Ibid.
66 Ibid 47.
67 Ibid.
68 Parliament of Australia, 'Family Assistance Legislation Amendment (More Help for Families—Increased Payments) Bill 2004', *Parliament of Australia* (Web Page) <https://parlinfo.aph.gov.au/parlInfo/search/display/display.w3p;query=Id%3A%22legislation%2Fbillhome%2Fr2044%22>.

2006 and $5,000 in July 2008. When introducing this policy, federal treasurer Peter Costello famously encouraged Australians to 'have one (child) for the father, one for the mother and one for the country'.[69] The introduction of policies like this one, prior to the commencement of a universal paid parental leave scheme, solidifies the premise that the government's focus was on motherhood and fertility instead of women's workforce participation. Again, the policy revolved around the cultural feminism approach, which celebrates motherhood and women's ability to reproduce. However, as the following section will address, this policy has been problematic for women since it did not readily aim for women's workforce participation. The policy contributed to the employment gap between men and women, effectively viewing women in a domestic role. The combination of the highly 'masculinised' industrial scene in Australia and the maternity allowances handed out by the government meant that maternity leave lagged as an industrial relations agenda item until female participation in the workforce increased.[70] Although historical cases sought equal workforce treatment between men and women,[71] in terms of leave, men and women were treated differently. In particular, mothers and carers were granted leave for bearing children; however, there was no monetary compensation.[72]

2 *Public Industries*

Historically, federal public servants were the first to receive employer-paid parental leave through the *Maternity Leave (Commonwealth Employees) Act 1973*.[73] This Act provided 12 weeks of paid maternity leave to federal public servants.[74] Over time, state governments also introduced employer-paid parental leave. For instance, the Northern Territory Government offers between 14 and 18 weeks of paid maternity leave, which is proportionate to the length of service.[75]

---

69 Misa Han, 'Peter Costello's "Baby Bonus" Generation Grows Up', *Australian Financial Review* (online 1 September 2017) <https://www.afr.com/politics/peter-costellos-baby-bonus-generation-grows-up-20170831-gy7wfg>.

70 Baird (n 160) 47.

71 See *Maternity Leave Case* (1979) 218 CAR 120.

72 Baird (n 160) 53.

73 *Maternity Leave (Commonwealth Employees) Act 1973* (Cth).

74 Ibid.

75 Office of the Commissioner for Public Employment, 'Northern Territory Public Sector 2017–2021 Enterprise Agreement' (Office of the Commissioner for Public Employment, 2017) 37 <https://ocpe.nt.gov.au/__data/assets/pdf_file/0010/460828/NTPS-2017-2021-Full-Enterprise-Agreement-Access-Period.pdf>.

Modern awards have set the standard for terms and conditions of employment in Australia.[76] In 2002, 82 federal awards provided for paid maternity leave, 59 of these from the government sphere, including education, health and local government.[77] By 2005, only 6% of modern awards provided for paid maternity leave that mirrored the 12-week federal public sector legislation.[78] An analysis of awards undertaken in 2005 suggested a clear pattern towards paid maternity leave in the federal public sector.[79] For example, a paid maternity leave period of 12 weeks was provided for by the Commonwealth and Victorian Governments and related employees through 75 awards.[80] The Communications, Electrical, Electronic, Energy, Information, Postal, Plumbing and Allied Services Union of Australia (Federal Electricians) paid employees eight weeks of paid maternity leave from 15 awards.[81] For journalists and auto-assembly employees, 14 awards provided for six weeks of paid maternity leave.[82] Some awards prescribed eligibility criteria regarding the length of service before maternity leave or an agreement to carry on with normal duties following the leave period.[83] The state public sector also reflected public sector legislation in a small number of public sector awards.[84] For example, an examination of NSW Industrial Gazettes in 2005 revealed that paid maternity leave appeared in 60 NSW awards, in particular awards for Crown employees, Catholic Church employees, local government and state utilities employees.[85] Like the federal jurisdiction, these state awards fell within the public sector, which could be attributed to the influence of the NSW state legislation mirrored by these awards.[86]

---

76 Baird (n 160) 53.
77 Department of Employment and Workplace Relations, Department of the Prime Minister and Cabinet and Department of Family and Community Services, Submission No 20 to Senate Employment, Workplace Relations and Education Legislation Committee, *Inquiry into the Workplace Relations Amendment (Paid Maternity Leave)* (26 July 2002).
78 Baird (n 160) 54.
79 Ibid.
80 Ibid.
81 Ibid.
82 Ibid.
83 Ibid 55.
84 Ibid.
85 Ibid.
86 Ibid.

3 Private Industries

At the start of the 21st century, three landmark events galvanized paid parental leave to be recognised as a principal agenda of industrial unions.[87] First, in 2000, the ILO introduced the C183, which stipulated a 14-week paid parental leave period,[88] together with the corresponding R191, which stipulated an 18-week paid parental leave period.[89] In the following year, the Australian Catholic University introduced a 12-week 100% and 40-week 60% wage replacement form of paid parental leave in their general staff academic agreement.[90] Finally, in 2002, the Human Rights and Equal Opportunity Commission launched an inquiry into Australian paid parental leave scheme proposals.[91] The decision of the Australian Catholic University ignited a series of enterprise bargaining claims calling for significant increases in parental leave within the tertiary sector, commencing new community benchmarks.[92]

Notwithstanding the publicity received by the enterprise bargaining arrangements on paid maternity leave in the early 21st century, entitlements remained stagnant.[93] Towards the end of 2003, only 10% of enterprise agreements included paid maternity leave, with only 7% of private-sector employers offering paid maternity leave in their agreements.[94] The ILO recommendation of 18 weeks of paid maternity leave[95] is barely achieved in most Australian enterprise agreements. At the time of writing, six and 12 weeks appear to be the dominant duration in most enterprise agreements.

In some sectors, recent developments in paid maternity leave under enterprise bargaining demonstrate further improvements in the overall

---

87 Ibid 57.

88 *Maternity Protection Convention, 2000 (No. 183)* (n 87).

89 *Maternity Protection Recommendation, 2000 (No. 191)* (n 88).

90 Denise Thompson, Michael Bittman and Peter Saunders, *The Impact of the Australian Catholic University's Paid Maternity Leave Provision: Final Report* (Social Policy Research Centre, UNSW, Publication Place: Sydney, 2004).

91 Human Rights and Equal Opportunity Commission, *Pregnant and Productive: It's a Right Not a Privilege to Work While Pregnant* (Report of the National Pregnancy and Work Inquiry, Australian Human Rights Commission, 2001) <https://humanrights. gov.au/our-work/pregnant-and-productive-its-right-not-privilege-work-while-pregnant-1999>.

92 Baird (n 160) 57.

93 Ibid.

94 Ibid.

95 *Maternity Protection Recommendation, 2000 (No. 191)* (n 88).

entitlements, for example, in higher education. At the time of writing, the current Menzies School of Health Research Enterprise Agreement provides for a total of 16 weeks paid parental leave (increased from the former 14-week period in its 2015 agreement)[96] for employees with 12 consecutive months of service.[97] The leave can be taken for 16 weeks at full pay or 32 weeks at half pay. Before a child's birth, employees are eligible to use personal or sick leave for antenatal care.[98] Any request by an employee on parental leave to return to work on a part-time basis will be reasonably considered by Menzies.[99]

Emerging trends on the increasing proportion of large organisations with paid parental leave provisions have also been identified through regular surveys conducted by the Workplace Gender Equity Agency ('WGEA'). The most recent report by the WGEA noted that, for the first time since the report's inception, over 50% of employers in their dataset provided access to paid parental leave on top of the statutory paid parental leave scheme.[100] In 2019–2020, the number of employers offering paid parental leave for primary carers increased to 52.4%, translating to approximately seven out of 10 employees in the WGEA dataset having access to paid parental leave for primary carers.[101] Women accounted for 93.5% of the primary carer's leave utilised, with men accounting for only 6.5%.[102] The most common duration for leave was 7–12 weeks, offered by 21.3% of employers, with only 4.7% of employers offering the ILO-recommended 18 weeks or more for primary carer's leave. In terms of the percentage of organisations offering primary carer's leave by industry, leave was most commonly offered by Electricity, Gas, Water and Waste Services (80.9%), Financial and Insurance Services (80.8%) and Education and Training (79.7%).[103] Agriculture, Forestry and Fishing industries sat at 37.9%, whereas Accommodation and Food Services (24.7%)

---

96 Menzies School of Health Research, 'Menzies School of Health Research Enterprise Agreement 2018' (Fairwork Commission, 29 January 2019) 29 <https://www.fwc.gov.au/documents/documents/agreements/fwa/ae501501.pdf>.

97 Ibid.

98 Ibid cl 6.5.4.

99 Ibid cl 6.7.7.

100 Workplace Gender Equality Agency, *Australia's Gender Equality Scorecard: Key Results from the Workplace Gender Equality Agency's 2019–20 Reporting Data* (November 2020) 11 <https://www.wgea.gov.au/sites/default/files/documents/2019-20%20Gender%20 Equality%20Scorecard_FINAL.pdf>.

101 Ibid.

102 Ibid.

103 Ibid 12.

and Retail Trade (24.0%) were the industries with the lowest percentage of employers offering primary carers leave.[104]

As discussed in the foregoing, the after-effects of negotiations set a benchmark for other players within the industry to follow. In the absence of enterprise agreements, parental leave outcomes remained at a bare minimum as confined within industry awards.[105] Professor Marian Baird argued that parental leave was viewed as a welfare issue instead of an employment issue for most of the 20th century,[106] which has been one of the underlying reasons why the surge of parental leave as part of the industrial relations agenda has lagged. Further, the male breadwinner model induced a lack of sensitivity to mainstream industrial relations discussions about women's workforce participation.[107] The earlier model of welfare payments is an example of cultural feminism at its best; however, it caused a delay in recognising women's unique roles in society as both mothers and providers. The introduction of the paid parental leave in industrial relations is leaning more towards the reconstructive feminism model, which helps women achieve the unique roles they hold within their families and society.

C Domestic Laws

1 Fairwork Act

The National Employment Standards ('NES') refer to the 'minimum standards that apply to the employment of national system employees'.[108] These standards relate to a myriad of employment matters,[109] including parental leave and related entitlements.[110] All provisions of employment contracts, awards or agreements must not be less than what is prescribed by the NES. For example, employees' minimum wage cannot be less than the national minimum wage prescribed by the NES,[111] which is currently $19.84 per hour.[112] The NES aids the establishment of minimum entitlements for unpaid parental leave and other related entitlements.[113] In addition to birth and adoption-related

---

104 Ibid.
105 Baird (n 160) 58.
106 Ibid.
107 Ibid.
108 *Fairwork Act 2009* (n 158) s 61(1).
109 Ibid s 61(2).
110 Ibid s 61(2)(c).
111 Ibid s 282.
112 Australian Government Fair Work Ombudsman (n 134).
113 *Fairwork Act 2009* (n 158) s 70.

provisions, other related entitlements include unpaid special parental leave,[114] 'no safe job leave' or safe job transferrals if applicable,[115] return-to-work guarantees[116] and unpaid pre-adoption leave.[117]

According to the *Fairwork Act 2009*, all employees who have worked with their employer for at least 12 months are entitled to take unpaid parental leave when they or their spouse/de facto partner gives birth or adopts a child.[118] The period of unpaid parental leave can be up to 12 months, with the option to request an additional 12 months,[119] bringing the total of unpaid parental leave of up to two years. Should an employee request the additional 12 months of leave, the request must be in writing and given to the employer at least four weeks before the end of the initial 12-month period.[120]

In addition, eligible employees who undertook unpaid parental leave have a return-to-work guarantee.[121] Employees are eligible to return to their 'pre-parental leave position' or if the former position no longer exists, 'an available position for which the employee is qualified and suited nearest in status and pay to the pre-parental leave position'.[122]

Since the passage of the *Fairwork Act 2009*, the Greens have intensely advocated on the issue of paid parental leave, remarking that the government is making false representations of working families by failing to legislate on a statutory paid parental leave scheme.[123] Liberal politician and Deputy Leader of the Opposition, Julie Bishop, commented on the release of the Productivity Commission report[124] shortly after the introduction of the *Fairwork Act 2009*. Bishop claimed that paid parental leave was at 'the very heart of our policy review on social and employment issues' and that the Coalition had a history of ongoing support for practical measures to help families with their responsibilities of raising children.[125] Contrarily, Senior Opposition member

---

114 Ibid s 80.
115 Ibid ss 81–82A.
116 Ibid s 84.
117 Ibid s 85.
118 Ibid s 70.
119 Ibid s 76.
120 Ibid.
121 Ibid s 84.
122 Ibid.
123 Jennifer Waterhouse and Linda Colley, 'The Work-Life Provisions of the Fair Work Act: A Compromise of Stakeholder Preference' (2010) 36(2) *Australian Bulletin of Labour* 154, 169.
124 Julie Bishop, 'Coalition Welcomes Productivity Commission Paid Parental Leave Report' (9 October 2008).
125 Ibid.

Tony Abbott reluctantly admitted that he was not in favour of a universal paid parental leave scheme, proclaiming that the Baby Bonus was already a form of paid parental leave, notwithstanding a person's employment status.[126]

2 Sex Discrimination Act

The *Sex Discrimination Act 1984*[127] makes it unlawful to discriminate against a person based on their sex, gender identity, intersex status, sexual orientation, marital or relationship status, family responsibilities, pregnancy or potential to become pregnant, or if that person is breastfeeding.[128] In the absence of any valid medical or safety reasons, pregnant women should not be barred from conducting their work in the same manner and under the same conditions as any other employee.[129] Similar to the provisions of the *Fairwork Act 2009*, the *Sex Discrimination Act 1984* also provides for the right of an employee to return to the position they held before commencing parental leave or to a comparable position should the original job have been made redundant.[130]

Direct pregnancy discrimination occurs when a woman is treated less favourably than another person because of her pregnancy or potential pregnancy.[131] Examples of direct discrimination by an employer include reduction of working hours allocated to a pregnant employee because of assumptions of fatigue; interviewing female job applicants about their plans to have children and subsequently disqualifying those who intend to start a family; and terminating or making pregnant employees redundant because of future absence from the workplace on parental leave.

Indirect pregnancy discrimination occurs when there is a workplace requirement or practice that applies equally to all employees but has a discriminatory effect on pregnant or potentially pregnant women. It arises where a person imposes or proposes to impose a condition, requirement or practice that can or is likely to disadvantage pregnant or potentially pregnant women,[132] which is unreasonable in the circumstances.[133] An example of indirect pregnancy discrimination is having a policy that only enables promotion after

---

126 'Steve Price with Tony Abbott, Federal Shadow Minister for Families, Housing, Community Services and Indigenous Affairs', *Morning* (Radio 2UE, 15 April 2009).
127 *Sex Discrimination Act 1984* (Cth).
128 Ibid s 14.
129 Ibid.
130 Ibid s 14.
131 Ibid s 14.
132 Ibid s 7(2).
133 Ibid s 7B.

two consecutive years of service since it indirectly discriminates against female employees who have broken their consecutive service by taking parental leave. In *Hickie v Hunt & Hunt*,[134] a female solicitor who was nominated for promotion to contract partner informed the firm that she was pregnant. A month later, it was agreed that the solicitor would take parental leave in the form of three months off work, followed by a three-day workweek on her return.[135] Just before the solicitor's scheduled return, a number of partners from the firm held a meeting with the solicitor wherein they suggested that she lessen her practice and surrender some of her current matters.[136] The solicitor rejected this proposal, which was followed by the firm's denial of her request for a temporary replacement.[137] The solicitor returned to work three days in the office and two days from home per week.[138] The solicitor received an unfavourable performance assessment, which purported that she was unable to run a practice and serve clients on a part-time basis, and her partnership contract was subsequently not renewed.[139] The solicitor claimed that the statement concerning part-time work was inherently a requirement that she must work full-time to keep her position and that such a requirement was a form of indirect discrimination based on sex.[140] The firm responded that full-time work was indeed inevitable for the position.[141] The commission held that the full-time work requirement would naturally disadvantage female practitioners, emphasising that such a requirement imposed on the solicitor to keep her position was unreasonable given the circumstances.[142] In addition, the commission noted the importance of the firm having clear parameters concerning maternity leave and part-time work policies to ensure that the minimum standards of fair and equal treatment were met.[143]

An employee returning from maternity leave may wish to work part-time or on a job-share basis, and the refusal of such request by an employer may be deemed discriminatory. In *Federal Municipal Shire and Shire Council Employee's Union of Australia (NSW) v Nambucca Shire Council*,[144] an employee relied on the

---

134 *Hickie v Hunt & Hunt* [1998] EOC 92-910.

135 Ibid.

136 Ibid.

137 Ibid.

138 Ibid.

139 Ibid.

140 Ibid.

141 Ibid.

142 Ibid.

143 Ibid.

144 *Federated Municipal and Shire Council Employee's Union of Australia (NSW) v Nambucca Shire Council* [1998] NSW IRC 6771.

provisions of an award that allowed job-sharing arrangements by agreement and made a request to that effect. The employer rejected the request based on the efficiency of such an arrangement.[145] The NSW Industrial Relations Commission held that women acting as primary carers to children might need to seek flexible work arrangements to cater for their caring responsibilities.[146] It was held that the employer's decision was indirectly discriminatory against the employee based on sex; therefore, the commissioner recommended that the employer trial a job-share arrangement.[147] Similarly, in *Bogle v Metropolitan Health Service Board*,[148] a dental clinic charge nurse requested a return to work on a part-time job share following a period of adoption leave. Her employer rejected her request and offered her old job full-time or a part-time job holding lesser status and responsibility as an alternative.[149] According to the employer, the charge nurse's position could not be shared, and the position had consistently been performed on a full-time basis.[150] However, the tribunal held that the requirement to work full-time imposed on employees with managerial roles adversely affected women and employees with family responsibilities.[151] The requirement was held to be unreasonable because the employer failed to conduct any reasonable analysis or evaluation of the employee's job-sharing proposal.[152]

---

145 Ibid.
146 Ibid.
147 Ibid.
148 *Bogle v Metropolitan Health Service Board* [2000] EOC 93-069.
149 Ibid.
150 Ibid.
151 Ibid.
152 Ibid.

Chapter 4

PAID MATERNITY AND PARENTAL LEAVE IN COMPARABLE OECD COUNTRIES

This section compares three OECD member countries with comparable GDP (total, US dollars per capita) to Australia (USD55,627) in 2021.[1] These OECD member countries are Canada (USD50,722), Germany (USD58,663) and Sweden (USD59,576). This comparison is restricted to paid maternity and parental leave provisions, with particular attention to leave duration, funding and eligibility. For ease of comparison, local currencies were converted to the equivalent Australian dollar amount.

Gross domestic product ('GDP') is the standard measure of a country's value created by the production of goods and services in that country for a particular period.[2] GDP also measures the income earned from such production or the total amount spent on final goods and services (less imports).[3] Although GDP is the single most important indicator to capture economic activity, it falls short of providing an appropriate measure of people's material well being for which alternative indicators may be more appropriate.[4] For example, analysing social welfare and employment benefits is not entirely dependent on GDP since GDP substantially focuses on economic growth. Therefore, this comparison will use 'nominal GDP' (or GDP at current prices or GDP in value) as an alternative indicator referring to US dollars per capita for the year 2021.

---

1 OECD Data 'Gross domestic product (GDP)(indicator)', *Organisation for Economic Co-operation and Development* (Web Page, 2021) <https://data.oecd.org/gdp/gross-domestic-product-gdp.htm>.
2 Ibid.
3 Ibid.
4 Ibid.

A Canada

As of 01 January 2022, Canadian entitlements available to mothers (maternity and parental leave combined) add to a maximum of 55 weeks paid at a full-time equivalent of CAD638 [AUD682] per week. The duration can be extended to a maximum of 84 weeks with a weekly payment of CAD638 [AUD682] for the first 15 weeks, followed by a weekly payment of CAD383 [AUD409] per week for the remaining 69 weeks.

In Canada, paid parental and maternity leave is administered through the Employee Insurance ('EI') program, enshrined in the *Employment Insurance Act*.[5] The EI Program is managed by the federal Department of Employment and Social Development and is available to all Canadian residents, except Quebec residents, who are covered by Quebec's parental leave program. Under the EI Program, benefits are funded by premiums paid by employers and employees, based on a premium rate that applies to every CAD100 [AUD107] of insurable earnings to the maximum insurable earnings threshold as determined by the Employment Insurance Financing Board annually.[6] The Act defines 'insurable earnings' as the total amount of earnings an insured person has from insurable employment.[7] Employees pay an EI premium rate of CAD1.58 [AUD1.69] per CAD100 [AUD107], with an annual EI premium maximum payment by employees of CAD952.74 [AUD1018].[8] Employers pay 1.4 times more than employee premiums, in particular, CAD2.21 [AUD2.37] per CAD100 [AUD107] insurable earnings.[9] Self-employed individuals can also be eligible to receive EI Program benefits by paying premiums similar to employees at CAD1.58 [AUD1.69] per CAD100 [AUD107] of insurable earnings up to the maximum insurable amount of earnings annually.[10] EI Program benefits are taxable.[11] As of 01 January 2022, the maximum insurable amount

---

5   *Employment Insurance Act*, SC 1996, c 23.

6   Employment and Social Development Canada, 'Employment Insurance - Important Notice about Maximum Insurable Earnings for 2022', *Government of Canada* (26 October 2021) <https://www. https://www.canada.ca/en/employment-social-development/programs/ei/ei-list/ei-employers/2022-maximum-insurable-earnings.html>.

7   *Employment Insurance Act*, SC 1996, c 23 (n 254) 2.

8   Employment and Social Development Canada (n 255).

9   Ibid.

10   Andrea Doucet et al, 'Canada Country Note' in Alison Koslowski et al (eds), *16ᵗʰ International Review of Leave Policies and Related Research 2020* (FernUniversität, 2020) 148 <https://www.leavenetwork.org/annual-review-reports/review-2020/>.

11   Ibid.

is CAD60,300 [AUD64431]; hence, the maximum payment is equivalent to a weekly rate of CAD638 [AUD682].[12] Paid parental and maternity leave provided for under the EI Program is referred to as 'benefits', while unpaid parental leave provided for under corresponding state and federal labour laws is referred to as 'leave'. This section focuses on Canada's benefit as of 01 January 2022; however, this monograph will not address Quebec's provisions.

To be eligible for paid benefits, a parent must have worked in insurable employment for 600 hours in the previous 52 weeks or since their last EI claim. Outside Quebec, self-employed individuals are eligible if they register in advance for the EI Special Benefit program, have paid premiums for at least one year and earned a minimum of CAD7,279 [AUD7,794] for claims filed in the preceding year. Non-citizens and migrant workers with a valid social insurance number and who meet other eligibility criteria may be eligible for maternity and parental benefits.[13]

1 Maternity Leave

EI maternity benefits are available to biological mothers, including surrogate mothers, who cannot work because of pregnancy or childbirth.[14] The maximum duration of the benefit is 15 weeks, with the first week being served as a 'waiting period'.[15] Payment of benefits is at a rate of 55% of the average insurable earnings up to the maximum insurable amount of CAD60,300 [AUD64,431].[16] Hence, maternity benefits are paid at a maximum rate of CAD638 [AUD683] per week for 15 weeks.

All maternity leave benefits must be exhausted by 17 weeks after the week in which the mother was expected to give birth or actually gave birth.[17] Receipt of maternity benefit may be delayed or extended by the amount of time a newborn is hospitalised; however, maternity benefits must be

---

12 Employment and Social Development Canada, 'Employment Insurance Maternity and Parental Benefits', *Government of Canada* (31 December 2020) <https://www.canada.ca/en/employment-social-development/programs/ei/ei-list/reports/maternity-parental.html>.

13 Service Canada, 'Maternity and Parental Leave Benefits', *Government of Canada* (Web Page, 2020) <https://www.canada.ca/en/services/benefits/ei/ei-maternity-parental/eligibility.html>.

14 *Employment Insurance Act*, SC 1996, c 23 (n 254) s 22(1).

15 Ibid s 22(2).

16 Ibid.

17 Ibid s 22(2)(b).

received within 52 weeks of the birth.[18] Maternity benefits may be combined with regular benefits in the event of job loss or with other special benefits such as parental benefits, sickness benefits, compassionate care benefits or family caregiver benefits for adults or parents of seriously ill children up to a maximum of 102 weeks (with proof of eligibility for the latter benefits).[19]

2 Parental Leave

Benefit payments under the EI Program may be claimed by either parent or can also be shared, subject to eligibility.[20] EI parental benefits are offered to parents who are caring for a newborn or newly adopted child or children.[21] Parental leave may be taken by either parent in either 'standard' or 'extended' form. The standard form provides up to 35 weeks of wage replacement per family at the same rate as maternity leave, which is 55% of the average insured earnings up to a maximum of CAD60,300 [AUD64,431] and is equivalent to CAD638 [AUD682] per week.[22] One or both parents can elect to share parental leave benefits in the extended form for up to 61 weeks by spreading the same benefit amount over prolonged periods, in particular, 61 weeks at 33% of earnings up to the maximum or a benefit payment ceiling of CAD383 [AUD409] per week.[23]

On 17 March 2019, the Parental Sharing Benefit was introduced, which provides an additional five weeks of benefits (under the standard form, extending benefits to 40 weeks) or an additional eight weeks (under the extended form, extending benefits to 69 weeks) when both parents undertake leave and obtain benefits under the EI Program.[24] This program aims to improve gender equality by motivating more fathers to participate in the uptake of parental leave.[25] Further, this program aims to promote the inclusion of all types of families, in particular families with same-sex partners and adoptive parents.[26] The additional five or eight weeks are restricted to parents of children born or adopted by them on or after 17 March 2019.[27]

---

18 Ibid s 22(7).
19 Doucet et al (n 259) 149.
20 Employment and Social Development Canada, 'Parental Sharing Benefit', *Government of Canada* (Web Page, 18 March 2019) <https://www.canada.ca/en/employment-social-development/campaigns/ei-improvements/parent-sharing.html>.
21 *Employment Insurance Act*, SC 1996, c 23 (n 254) s 23(1).
22 Ibid s 23(4.1)(a).
23 Ibid s 23(4.1)(b).
24 Employment and Social Development Canada (n 269).
25 Ibid.
26 Ibid.
27 Ibid.

B Germany

German entitlements available to mothers (maternity and parental leave combined) add to a maximum of 76 weeks paid at a full-time equivalent of approximately €400 [AUD673] per week. The duration can be extended to a maximum of 120 weeks with a weekly payment of €200 [AUD315].

In Germany, the *Mutterschutzgesetz*[28] governs paid maternity leave, providing benefits to mothers following pregnancy and childbirth and affording mothers protection against unlawful termination from work during pregnancy until four months after childbirth. In addition, the *Bundeselterngeld-und Elternzeitgesetz*[29] governs paid parental leave, divided into two sections, namely, 'Elternzeit', which refers to job protection rights and the right to work part-time, and 'Basiselterngeld' and 'ElterngeldPlus', which refer to parental benefits.

1 Maternity Leave

Maternity leave ('Mutterschutz') is available to mothers for a mandatory period of 16 weeks. The leave is divided into two periods, the first being the last eight weeks before childbirth or the 'presumed date of confinement'.[30] The 'eight-week period' is calculated based on a medical certificate, and in the event of childbirth being earlier or later than the stipulated date, the period will be shortened or extended accordingly.[31] The second period is the first eight weeks following childbirth, extended to 12 weeks in the event of premature births, multiple births or Caesarean section births.[32] Should the portion of the 'eight-week period' before childbirth be cut short, the missing time is added to the period following childbirth, which must not exceed 16 weeks.[33] In addition to the mandatory maternity leave, mothers are protected from job dismissal from week 12 of pregnancy until four months following childbirth (including stillbirths).[34]

Payments during maternity leave are referred to as 'Mutterschaftsgeld' or maternity leave benefits, paid at a rate of 100% of the mother's average

28 *Gesetz zum Schutz von Müttern bei der Arbeit, in der Ausbildung und im Studium (Mutterschutzgesetz - MuSchG)* [Maternity Protection Act] (Germany) 1979, FLG 1228.

29 *Bundeselterngeld - und Elternzeitgesetz - BEEG* [Parental Allowances and Parental Leave Act] (Germany) 05 December 2006, BGBI I.S, 2748.

30 *Gesetz zum Schutz von Müttern bei der Arbeit, in der Ausbildung und im Studium (Mutterschutzgesetz - MuSchG)* [Maternity Protection Act] (Germany) 1979, FLG s 3(1).

31 Ibid s 3(2).

32 Ibid s 5(1).

33 Ibid s 5(1).

34 Ibid s 10(1).

monthly income for the preceding three months prior to the commencement of maternity leave or 'previous earnings'.[35] Although these benefits are funded by the mother's health insurance,[36] employers play a vital role in paying maternity benefits. Since 2006, employers have been required to pay a premium to women's health insurance at a rate of approximately 0.2% of the gross salary of their female employees.[37] If there is a discrepancy between the maternity benefit from the insurance and the mother's payable benefits, the employer pays the difference to cover 100% of the mother's previous earnings.[38] The payment to mothers is directly made by the employer, who is subsequently eligible to apply for reimbursement at the appropriate health insurance institution.[39] Benefits for mothers with a monthly income below €390 [AUD615] are solely paid by the mother's health insurance, matching their prior income.[40] Benefits are also payable to mothers receiving unemployment benefits, wherein their health insurance matches their unemployment benefits.[41] Self-employed and unemployed mothers (not receiving unemployment benefits) who do not hold public health insurance have no maternity benefits payable to them; however, they may apply for up to €210 [AUD331] per month, paid for by the state social security.[42]

Subject to meeting the residency and employment contract requirements, all female employees (including part-time employees and employees who work below the statutory social insurance threshold at €450 [AUD710] per month), students and pupils, female voluntary workers, self-employed women and asylum seekers are eligible to receive maternity benefits.[43] In the case of students and pupils, female voluntary workers, self-employed women and asylum seekers who are secured by family or private insurance as opposed to public health insurance, a minimum monthly maternity benefit of €210 [AUD331] is payable.[44] It is unlawful to deport asylum seekers out of Germany for the duration of pregnancy and maternity leave.[45]

---

35 Ibid s 14(1).
36 Pia Schober et al, 'Germany Country Note' in Alison Koslowski et al (eds), *16th International Review of Leave Policies and Related Research 2020* (FernUniversität, 2020) 275 <https://www.leavenetwork.org/annual-review-reports/review-2020/>.
37 Ibid.
38 Ibid.
39 Ibid.
40 Ibid.
41 Ibid.
42 Ibid 278.
43 Ibid 276.
44 Ibid.
45 Ibid.

2 Parental Leave

In addition to maternity leave, parental leave can be taken by parents (mothers or fathers) for up to three years after childbirth for each parent, 24 months of which can be taken up until the child's eighth birthday.[46] Job protection is available to all employees while on parental leave, and they are entitled to the same working hours upon their return.[47] This period of absence from work is commonly referred to as Elternzeit, wherein parents do not receive a salary while on leave. However, parental benefits in the form of Basiselterngeld or ElterngeldPlus is payable throughout a substantial duration of the parental leave.[48] There is an option for the mother or father to take extended parental leave for a total of 24 months, with a parental allowance of €300 to €1,200 (depending on salary), paid by the government for the initial 14 months. The federal government funds the parental leave benefits through general taxation.[49]

To be eligible for parental leave, all parents must have been employed at the date of birth and should not be employed more than 30 hours per week while on parental leave.[50] The following people are eligible to receive parental benefits: all parents working 0–30 hours per week who are living in the same household with the child (this includes separated parents with joint custody); other people caring for the child when parents are ill, disabled, or dead; adoptive parents and foster parents; self-employed parents; same-sex couples; parents with a net income equal to or less than €500,000 [AUD 788,590] or a single parent with an income equal to or less than €250,000 [AUD394,295]; citizens of the European Union, European Economic Area and Switzerland if they are employed in Germany or live in Germany (according to European Union legislation); citizens of other countries with a permanent residence permit or with a working contract in Germany; asylum seekers who have lived in Germany for at least three years.[51]

On confirmation of eligibility, parents can take either full-time leave with a corresponding parental benefit (Basiselterngeld) or part-time leave with a corresponding parental benefit (ElterngeldPlus). These payments are income-related and can be combined if the parent wishes to do so.

---

46 *Bundeselterngeld - und Elternzeitgesetz - BEEG* [Parental Allowances and Parental Leave Act] (Germany) 05 December 2006, BGBI I.S, art 16(1).

47 Ibid art 18.

48 Ibid art 2.

49 Schober et al (n 285) 278.

50 *Bundeselterngeld - und Elternzeitgesetz - BEEG* [Parental Allowances and Parental Leave Act] (Germany) 05 December 2006, BGBI I.S, art 15.

51 Ibid art 1.

If parents take full-time leave to care for their child, they can receive Basiselterngeld for 12 months following childbirth.[52] This full-time benefit is paid at a rate of 65% of the preceding year's net earnings with a minimum of €300 [AUD473] per month and a maximum of €1,800 [AUD2,839] per month.[53] Under the Basiselterngeld option, parents receive an additional two months of benefits if both parents take at least two months of leave in the form of partner months or 'Partnermonate'.[54] However, maternity leave benefits paid during the eight-week obligatory maternity leave after childbirth is deducted from the total duration of Basiselterngeld, effectively reducing the benefit period for employed mothers to 10 months.[55]

Conversely, if parents take part-time leave, thereby reducing their work hours to care for their child, they are eligible to receive ElterngeldPlus for 24 months following childbirth.[56] This part-time benefit is paid at a rate of 65% of the preceding year's net earnings to compensate for lost earnings, with approximately half of ElterngeldPlus payments ranging between €150 [AUD237] and €900 [AUD1,420].[57] Under the ElterngeldPlus option, parents receive an additional four months of benefits as a partnership bonus or 'Partnerschaftsbonus' if both parents work part-time between 25 and 30 hours per week for at least four subsequent months.[58] However, maternity leave benefits paid during the eight-week obligatory maternity leave after childbirth is deducted from the total duration of ElterngeldPlus, effectively reducing the benefit period for employed mothers to 22 months.[59]

Parental leave entitlements are individual entitlements, with both parents having the option to receive their parental leave benefits simultaneously.[60] A supplementary payment for parents with more than one young child is also available in the form of 'Geschwisterbonus'. If there are two children under three years of age, or three or more children under six years of age, or two children of which at least one is disabled and under 14 years of age in the household, the parental benefit is expanded by 10% (at least €75 [AUD118] per child for Basiselterngeld or €37.50 [AUD59] for ElterngeldPlus).[61] In the event

---

52 Ibid art 2.
53 Ibid art 2.
54 Ibid art 2.
55 Ibid art 4d.
56 Ibid art 4.
57 Ibid art 4.
58 Ibid art 4.
59 Ibid art 4d.
60 Schober et al (n 285) 278.
61 *Bundeselterngeld - Und Elternzeitgesetz - BEEG* [Parental Allowances and Parental Leave Act] (Germany) 05 December 2006, BGBl I.S, art 2a.

of multiple births, another supplementary payment of €300 [AUD473] (Basiselterngeld) or €150 [AUD237] (ElterngeldPlus) per month is paid per additional child.[62]

C Sweden

Swedish entitlements available to mothers (maternity and parental leave combined) add to a maximum of 92 weeks paid at a full-time equivalent of SEK4,710 [AUD780] per week for the first 14 weeks, followed by approximately SEK460 [AUD731] for 69 weeks and SEK180 [AUD140] for the remaining nine weeks.[63] Sweden has a long tradition of working towards gender equality. Gender equality means that women and men enjoy the same rights and opportunities in all areas of life, for example, equal opportunities in the labour market, shared responsibility for the home and children and economic equality. One important date in this respect was 1921 when women gained the right to vote.[64] Many reforms and laws have been introduced since that date.[65] In Sweden, there is one legislation concerning the right to leave (78 weeks)[66] governed by the Ministry of Enterprise and Innovation and a separate legislation granting benefits (48 weeks)[67] governed by the Ministry of Health and Social Affairs.

1 Maternity Leave

Pregnant women are entitled to 'graviditetspenning' or maternity leave for 14 weeks, with a mandatory leave period of two weeks before or after childbirth.[68] The leave is divided into two periods, the first being the seven weeks prior to the estimated time of delivery. The second period is the remaining seven

---

62 Ibid art 2a.
63 Ann-Zofie Duvander and Niklas Löfgren, 'Sweden Country Note' in Alison Koslowski et al (eds), *16ᵗʰ International Review of Leave Policies and Related Research 2020* (FernUniversität, 2020) 555, 555, 557–558 <https://www.leavenetwork.org/annual-review-reports/review-2020/>.
64 While Sweden was not the first country in this regard as Australian women were given the right to vote in 1902. New Zealand women gained the vote in 1893. Women in Canada and Germany also gained the right to vote ahead of Sweden.
65 Regeringskansliet, 'English - How Sweden Is Governed', *Regeringskansliet* (Web Page, 19 February 2016) <https://www.regeringen.se/other-languages/english---how-sweden-is-governed/>.
66 Swedish right to leave of 18 months converted into weeks.
67 Swedish benefits of 240 days converted into full-time work weeks.
68 *Föräldrapenning* [Parental Leave Act] (Sweden) 1995, 584 s 4.

weeks after the delivery.[69] During the leave period, women are entitled to paid parental insurance benefit provided by the Social Security Insurance Code.[70] If a job is deemed to be 'physically demanding' and a pregnant employee is unable to carry out her duties, the Swedish Social Insurance Agency can grant up to 50 days of leave during the remaining 60 days of pregnancy, paid at the pregnancy benefit rate of 77.6% of income.[71] Moreover, if a job poses a risk to the pregnant woman or unborn child, and there is no suitable alternative job, the pregnant woman may undertake an indefinite leave period at the same pregnancy benefit rate of 77.6% of income.[72] The pregnancy benefit is only payable subject to the female employee's provision of a physician's certificate validating claims to the effect of the foregoing.[73]

2 Parental Leave

In addition to maternity leave, each parent is entitled to receive a parental allowance or 'föräldrapenning' that allows for 18 months of full-time leave from work.[74] Leave is also available for reducing working hours or caring for an unwell child.[75] Parents holding joint custody are eligible for 240 days of 'parental leave benefits' each.[76] A total of 90 days of the parental leave benefits falls under the 'mother's quota' or 'father's quota', which is non-transferrable to the other parent and is reserved for the mother and father, respectively.[77] The remainder of the parental leave period, equivalent to 105 days, is transferable to the other parent by signing a consent form.[78] If a child has a sole parent or the other parent is permanently ill and unable to care for the child, then the 90-day quota is waived, allowing one parent to take the entirety of the parental leave benefits for a total of 480 days.[79] A parent who earns a lesser income during the child's

---

69 Ibid s 4.
70 *Socialförsäkringsbalk* [Social Insurance Code] (Sweden) 2010, 110 ch 10 s 2.
71 *Föräldrapenning* [Parental Leave Act] (Sweden) 1995, 584 s 19.
72 Ibid s 20.
73 Ann-Zofie Duvander and Niklas Löfgren, 'Sweden Country Note' in Alison Koslowski et al (eds), *16th International Review of Leave Policies and Related Research 2020* (FernUniversität, 2020) 555, 557–558 <https://www.leavenetwork.org/annual-review-reports/review-2020/>.
74 *Föräldrapenning* [Parental Leave Act] (Sweden) 1995, 584 s 3.
75 Ibid.
76 *Socialförsäkringsbalk* [Social Insurance Code] (Sweden) 2010, 110 ch 12 s 35(1).
77 Duvander and Löfgren (n 312) 558.
78 Ibid.
79 Ibid.

first four years receives additional benefits.[80] The additional benefits are aimed at compensating the parent's uptake of the largest responsibility for childcare, which requires the parent to lessen their work, or in some cases, temporarily exit the workforce.[81]

The payment of parental leave in Sweden is quite complex, with parental benefits being paid at three levels: sickness benefit level, basic level and minimum level. Sickness benefit level refers to the level of benefits paid to 'an insured person who has a reduced ability to work due to illness', and, inter alia, benefits calculated under the Social Insurance Code to provide pregnancy (or maternity) benefit and parental benefit.[82] Parental benefit at the level of sickness benefit may be paid to a parent who has had an income of over SEK250 [AUD39] per day for 240 days and has been insured for work-based parental benefit.[83] The current sickness benefit level is 77.6% of earnings.[84] Parental benefits paid at the basic level may be paid to a parent who is insured for residence-based parental benefit and is paid at a fixed rate of SEK250 [AUD39] per day.[85] Finally, the parental benefit paid at the minimum level may be paid to a parent who is insured for residence-paid parental benefit, and at the time, is not eligible to receive sickness benefit level or basic level and is paid at a flat rate of SEK180 [AUD28] per day.[86]

For parents eligible for an income-related benefit, more commonly referred to as sickness benefit level, 195 days of leave are paid at 77.6% of earnings up to a maximum of SEK465,000 [AUD72,609].[87] The remaining 45 days are paid at the minimum level, which is a flat-rate payment of SEK180 [AUD28] per day.[88] If the parent has been insured for at least 240 consecutive days before the child's birth or the estimated time of birth for sickness benefit, and during that time the parent would have been entitled to a sickness benefit that exceeds the minimum level, then the first 180 days of parental leave must be paid at the sickness benefit level at 77.6% of earnings.[89] If the preceding condition is not met, the parent will receive parental benefits at the basic level, receiving a flat rate of SEK250 [AUD39] per day for 240 days.[90]

---

80 Ibid.
81 Ibid.
82 *Socialförsäkringsbalk* [Social Insurance Code] (Sweden) 2010, 110 ch 24.
83 Ibid ch 12 s 21.
84 Ibid ch 28 s 7(1).
85 Ibid ch 12 s 22.
86 Ibid ch 12 s 24.
87 Ibid ch 12 s 21.
88 Ibid ch 12 s 23.
89 Ibid ch 12 s 35(1).
90 Ibid ch 12 s 35(2).

Chapter 5

CALL FOR LAW REFORM

The feminist theories have a strong role in the arguments for paid parental leave. Although liberal feminism has been identified as a strong foundation for women's rights, it has limitations in analysing paid parental leave policies because of the disregard of biological differences. If paid leave had been designed in line with this theory, it would have been enacted by the *Fairwork Act 2009* and provided up to two years of unpaid leave for both men and women on the birth or adoption of a child. Childbirth, recovery from childbirth and breastfeeding are biological realities that separate parents who adopt from those who do not. On the contrary, cultural feminism, which appreciates women's unique qualities, champions women's rights by celebrating the differences that liberal feminism chooses to ignore. An illustration of cultural feminism is the enactment of the *Paid Parental Leave Act 2010*, granting women 18 weeks of paid parental leave on the birth or adoption of a child. On the face of it, this arrangement appears to benefit women and is consistent with the most up-to-date ILO *Maternity Protection Convention No. 183*[1] and *Maternity Protection Recommendation No. 191*.[2] However, it falls short of meeting the 'best interests of the child' obligations set out by the CRC since it does not meet the 26-week minimum leave duration recommended by the WHO for optimal maternal and child health. Further, the minimum leave duration warrants women to choose between returning to work early or taking unpaid leave or even exiting the workforce to care for their infant for the recommended 26 weeks. Consequently, taking leave or exiting workplace might contribute to the discrimination against women because of family or carer responsibilities, as pointed out by the Law Council of Australia in their submission on the Fairer Paid Parental Leave Bill.[3] Since the 18-week statutory paid parental leave is exclusive to women, an assumption is made through the lens of cultural feminism that women are full-time caregivers and incapable of being long-term family providers.

---

1 *Maternity Protection Convention, 2000 (No. 183)* (entered into force 07 February 2002).
2 *Maternity Protection Recommendation, 2000 (No. 191)* (n 88).
3 Fairer Paid Parental Leave Bill 2016 (Cth).

Meanwhile, reconstructive feminism follows the premise that women need equality and argues that equality is achieved by stripping down social, often masculine norms that put women at a disadvantage. As examined in Chapter 2, one of the core reasons why working women's pregnancies and burdensome family responsibilities contribute to gender disparity is that society's definition of the standard worker is someone working full-time continuously for long periods, i.e. starting from 18 years old to 65-year-old with no career interruptions. Since society is heavily dominated by the masculine norm of working traditionally to provide financially, there is little room to accommodate the thought of women caring for young children while contributing financially to family and society. It is argued here that reconstructive feminism provides the most adequate view of women's needs surrounding childbirth or adoption compared with liberal or cultural feminism. As a result, suggestions for reform on Australian paid parental leave will be based on a reconstructive feminist viewpoint, one that guarantees women the pivotal right to full and equal participation in the workforce without being denied the basic right to full participation within the family.

A review of the literature identified substantial parental leave provisions through human rights treaties, in particular, the CEDAW[4], the ICESCR[5] and the CRC.[6] These treaties demonstrated a robust international foundation for the provision of paid parental leave in Australia. Further, the development of international standards in the form of ILO Conventions and Recommendations were explored. The inaugural *Maternity Protection Convention, 1919 (No. 3)*[7] introduced a 12-week minimum paid maternity leave provision in 1919, which developed into the *Maternity Protection Convention No. 183*[8] stipulating a 14-week minimum paid maternity leave provision to date. The *Maternity Protection Convention No. 183*[9] was accompanied by the *Maternity Protection Recommendation, 2000 (No. 191)*[10] extending the paid parental leave period to a minimum of

---

4 *Convention on the Elimination of All Forms of Discrimination against Women*, opened for signature 18 December 1979, 1249 UNTS 13 (entered into force 03 September 1981).

5 *International Covenant on Economic, Social and Cultural Rights*, opened for signature 16 December 1966, 993 UNTS 3 (entered into force 03 January 1976).

6 *Convention on the Rights of the Child*, opened for signature 20 November 1989, 1577 UNTS 3 (entered into force 02 September 1990).

7 *Maternity Protection Convention, 1919 (No. 3)* (n 77).

8 *Maternity Protection Convention, 2000 (No. 183)* (entered into force 07 February 2002).

9 Ibid.

10 *Maternity Protection Recommendation, 2000 (No. 191)* (n 88).

18 weeks. While Australia meets the 18-week minimum set by the current ILO Convention and Recommendation, there has been no significant improvement regarding extending the duration and increasing funding since the introduction of a statutory paid parental leave scheme in 2010. Although the Productivity Commission recommended a review of the scheme by the Australian Government three years after its inception on its effectiveness, influence on leave taken by parents and any modest changes to the duration of the scheme required,[11] there has been no further studies as extensive as the 2009 Productivity Commission Inquiry evaluating the effectiveness and adequacy of existing paid parental leave laws.

Considering the paid leave entitlements available to mothers through the feminist theory lenses, it becomes clear that Australia compares unfavourably with other OECD countries that have comparable nominal GDP. Table 5.1 illustrates that although the weekly benefit payments available in Australia, Canada, Germany and Sweden are broadly comparable, the number of weeks in total in which benefits are paid in Australia is considerably lower than the other countries.

In comparing paid leave entitlements among Canada, Germany and Sweden, two forms of paid parental leave were identified: maternity (or pregnancy) leave and parental leave. As mentioned in the literature, maternity leave primarily refers to women's entitlement to leave for pregnancy and childbirth. For example, both German Mutterschutz (16 weeks) and Swedish graviditetspenning (14 weeks) stipulate mandatory maternity leave periods divided into a period for pregnancy and a period following childbirth. Meanwhile, Canadian maternity benefits (15 weeks) are available to both biological and surrogate mothers who are deemed unable to work due to pregnancy or childbirth. Because of the specific purpose of these maternity leave provisions (for pregnancy and childbirth), it can be assumed that these policies fall within the cultural feminist approach. Although officially called 'paid parental leave', the Australian equivalent of these cultural feminist maternity leave policies is the statutory paid parental leave period of 18 weeks, exclusive to the 'birth mother' or 'primary carer'—identified to be mothers 95% of the time.[12] Maternity leave duration is comparable between Australia (18 weeks) and Canada, Germany and Sweden (ranging, on average, 15 weeks). However, the Australian payment is fixed at the national minimum wage, whereas the other three countries provide a wage replacement payment that averages 77.5% of previous earnings.

---

11 Productivity Commission (n 98) XLIV.
12 Australian Bureau of Statistics (n 3).

Table 5.1 Maximum paid leave entitlements in Australia, Canada, Germany and Sweden available to mothers

Country	Paid Maternity Leave		Paid Parental Leave		Total Paid Leave	
	Duration (weeks)	Amount (AUD per week)	Duration (weeks)	Amount (AUD per week)	Duration (weeks)	Amount (AUD per week)
Australia	0	0	18[13]	754	18[14]	754
Canada	15	682	35 + (5 extra weeks)[15]	682	55	682
Germany	16	636[16]	52 + (8 extra weeks)[17]	710	76	673[18]
Sweden	14	780[19]	78[20]	731 (for the first 69 weeks) 140 (9 weeks)[21]	92	780 (first 14 weeks) 731 (for 69 weeks following the initial 14-week period) 140 (for 9 weeks following the 69-week period)[22]

13 20 weeks were announced under Federal budget of 2022, with implementation from 1 July 2022.
14 20 weeks were announced under Federal budget of 2022, with implementation from 1 July 2022.
15 Additional five weeks in the standard form through Parental Sharing Benefit.
16 Maternity leave is paid at 100% replacement wages. For example, using the minimum wage (€1,614 per month) a weekly wage replacement of €403.50[AUD602] is applicable.
17 Additional eight weeks of benefits when both parents undertake parental leave.
18 Average of maternity and parental leave full-rate equivalent.
19 Maximum daily cap at SEK1,006[AUD144] a day.
20 480 days less 90 days father's quota converted to weeks (5 days per week).
21 Daily maximum payment at sickness benefit level is SEK942 per day. The ceiling for the maximum amount is reached at a salary of SEK465,000 per annum. The remaining 90 days is paid at SEK180 per day.
22 Daily maximum payment at sickness benefit level is SEK942 per day. The ceiling for the maximum amount is reached at a salary of SEK465,000 per annum. The remaining 90 days is paid at SEK180 per day.

Further, the OECD member countries featured here have parental leave policies that provide individual entitlements (available to mothers and fathers) following the birth or adoption of a child. These entitlements are often supplementary to statutory paid maternity leave periods. What is surprising is that despite the comparable nominal GDP of Australia, Canada, Germany and Sweden, Australian parental leave policies substantially lag compared with the aforementioned OECD member countries. In particular, Canada offers 'parental benefits' of up to 35 weeks paid at 55% of previous earnings, with an additional five weeks should both parents undertake parental leave.[23] Meanwhile, Germany offers Basiselterngeld of up to 48 weeks paid at 65% of previous earnings, with an additional eight weeks of benefits should both parents undertake parental leave.[24] Sweden offers föräldrapenning of up to 92 weeks,[25] paid at 77.6% of previous earnings for 75 weeks, followed by a fixed minimum level payment for the remaining 22 weeks.[26] In stark contrast, Australia does not have a separate paid parental leave scheme that is equally available for both parents, unlike the provisions of the featured OECD member countries. The closest entitlement to the foregoing is the statutory unpaid leave laws provided for by the *Fairwork Act 2009*, offering Australian mothers and fathers up to 24 months of unpaid leave following the birth or adoption of a child.

The results of the comparisons demonstrate that Australia and the featured OECD member countries afford equal rights, albeit the former providing unpaid leave while the latter provide paid leave to men and women caring for a newborn or newly adopted child. In this regard, liberal feminism trumps by advocating women's rights through dismissal of the differences between men and women. Further, Germany and Sweden offer additional periods of leave as an incentive for men's uptake of leave, assisting in bridging

23 Andrea Doucet et al, 'Canada Country Note' in Alison Koslowski et al (eds), *16th International Review of Leave Policies and Related Research 2020* (FernUniversität, 2020) 146, 152 <https://www.leavenetwork.org/annual-review-reports/review-2020/>.

24 Pia Schober et al, 'Germany Country Note' in Alison Koslowski et al (eds), *16th International Review of Leave Policies and Related Research 2020* (FernUniversität, 2020) 277–278 <https://www.leavenetwork.org/annual-review-reports/review-2020/>.

25 480 days of entitlements if combined, less 90 day-mandatory leave for the mother/father.

26 Ann-Zofie Duvander and Niklas Löfgren, 'Sweden Country Note' in Alison Koslowski et al (eds), *16th International Review of Leave Policies and Related Research 2020* (FernUniversität, 2020) 557–558 <https://www.leavenetwork.org/annual-review-reports/review-2020/>.

the gap in workforce equality between men and women. The main weakness, however, in Australia's arrangement is that although it offers comparable job protection to Canada, Germany and Sweden, it lacks the recognition of women as equally important providers by failing to confer equivalent paid parental leave entitlements. Meanwhile, the generous leave duration and payments in Canada, Germany and Sweden arguably give women the option to stay at home and still contribute financially to the household and society. By combining maternity and parental leave benefits, women in these countries are eligible for an average of 74 weeks of paid entitlements[27], approximately three-fold the WHO's recommended leave duration for optimal maternal and child health. Such a combination of leave gives rise to a reconstructive feminism paragon, where women's differences from men are celebrated (with more leave accounted for women because of their biological differences) but where social norms are stripped down by granting men and women an equivalent amount of paid leave to care for a newborn or newly adopted child. The arrangements in the featured OECD member countries respect women's unique role in society by affording them leave for pregnancy and childbirth and respecting their role as providers for the family, conferring sustainable periods of paid leave until the child is at least one year old. One may argue that a combination of Australian paid parental leave provisions (equivalent to maternity leave provisions elsewhere) and unpaid parental leave provisions (equivalent to parental leave provisions elsewhere) yield a similar reconstructive feminism result. However, the key problem with this argument is that Australia's lack of sufficient leave provision puts women in a difficult position following the statutory 18-week paid parental leave period. In the absence of employer-provided parental leave, the choice for Australian women are to go back to work earlier than they would have preferred (and generally before the baby turns six months old); remain on unpaid leave, thereby disrupting the family's cashflow and causing unnecessary financial restraint; or in some cases, completely leave the workforce.

Therefore, it is advocated to apply the reconstructive feminist approach to Australian paid parental leave. First, the objectives of the Act include caring for the child following childbirth or adoption and enhancing maternal and child health and development. Australia has accepted the responsibility of promoting the 'best interests' of the child by adopting the CRC, yet the 18-week[28] statutory paid parental leave provision falls short of the 26-week

---

27 74 weeks derived from getting the average of the maximum paid parental leave entitlements available to mothers in Canada (55 weeks), Germany (76 weeks) and Sweden (92 weeks).

28 Or 20 week period proposed from 1 July 2022.

Table 5.2 Proposal for reform in Australia

Country	Paid Maternity Leave		Paid Parental Leave		Total Paid Leave	
	Duration (weeks)	Amount (AUD per week)	Duration (weeks)	Amount (AUD per week)	Duration (weeks)	Amount (AUD per week)
Australia	15	754	37 weeks	754	52	754

minimum leave duration as recommended by the WHO for optimal maternal and child health. To bring some parity with the comparable countries, Australia will have to introduce paid maternity leave of 15 weeks, extend paid parental leave to 35 weeks and allow for two weeks Dad's or Partner's leave to be taken by non-primary carers (Table 5.2).

It is possible that these reforms have to be introduced in stages. The progressive paid parental leave policies of Canada, Germany and Sweden have successfully developed over time. In Canada, 10 weeks of paid parental leave was introduced in 1990; the duration was increased to 35 weeks a decade later, and since 2019 it has been extended to 40 weeks.[29] Germany introduced 16 weeks of full-time paid parental leave in 1968, progressively increasing it to 20 weeks in 1988, 26 weeks in 1989, 32 weeks in 1990, 44 weeks in 1993 and 52 weeks since 2007.[30] Meanwhile, Sweden introduced 24 weeks of full-time paid parental leave in 1974, progressively increasing it to 30 weeks in 1975, 36 weeks in 1978, 48 weeks in 1980, 60 weeks in 1989 and 69 weeks since 2002.[31] These trends demonstrate substantial advancements in paid parental leave laws within these countries; across all three countries, the current average duration of paid leave is 74 weeks,[32] which is approximately three-fold the WHO's recommendation for parental leave. In contrast, there has been no advancement in the duration and generosity of paid parental leave in Australia since its inception. In the interests of placing optimal maternal and child wellbeing at the core of Australia's statutory paid

---

29 OECD Family Database, *PF 2.5 Annex: Detail of Change in Parental Leave by Country* (OECD Family Database Indicators, Organisation for Economic Co-operation and Development, April 2021) 8 <https://www.oecd.org/els/family/PF2_5_Trends_in_ leave_entitlements_around_childbirth_annex.pdf>.

30 Ibid 10.

31 Ibid 60.

32 74 weeks derived from getting the average of the maximum paid parental leave entitlements available to mothers in Canada (55 weeks), Germany (76 weeks) and Sweden (92 weeks).

parental leave policy, an increase to the 18-week statutory paid parental leave period is recommended. In the first stage of reforms, the minimum duration of paid parental leave in Australia should be amended to at least 26 weeks, as recommended by the WHO, noting that 26 weeks still falls far short of the paid parental leave provisions of the featured OECD member countries.

Second, there are inconsistencies between the objectives of the *Paid Parental Leave Act 2010* and its practical application. The objectives of the Act also include encouraging women's workforce participation and promoting gender equality for women, yet its 'primary carer' stipulation is heavily geared towards women taking time off work, with 95% of primary carers being mothers. In 2017, less than half of women (42%) who had a child under two years of age had returned to work since the birth of their child.[33] This statistic contradicts the objective of the Act to promote gender equality in the workforce, given that despite the statutory paid parental leave, the majority of women had exited the workforce following childbirth or adoption. Of those women who returned to work, only one out of four women had spent at least 10 months at home with their child, while approximately three out of four women had spent at least four months at home with their child.[34] The four-month duration is consistent with the 18-week statutory paid parental leave provision, implying that the lack of paid parental leave after 18 weeks might be influencing women's decisions to return to work. Since sufficient leave in addition to the statutory 18-week period is unavailable, women are left to either stay at home or return to work earlier than the ideal 26-week period. This policy does not address gender inequality nor encourage women's workforce participation, where parental leave exclusive to mothers is made. Australia could either amend the *Paid Parental Leave Act 2010* to include an additional entitlement for mothers or legislate a 'Maternity Leave Act' to formally recognise the individual rights of mothers while also considering the unique needs of mothers regarding pregnancy and recovery from childbirth, like all maternity provisions in Canada, Germany, and Sweden. Following the WHO guidelines, a 26-week paid maternity leave period is recommended. Provided that the aforementioned recommendations are enacted, the most appropriate OECD reference point would be Germany. Germany's paid parental leave scheme is publicly funded by taxation, like Australia, and the clarity of legislation and simplified payment rates are easily understood, allowing for ease of reference by families planning to have a child or more children in future.

---

33 Australian Bureau of Statistics, *Pregnancy and Employment Transitions* (n 3).
34 Ibid.

Although this monograph focused on the majority of primary carers in Australia (95% being mothers), a note of caution is needed for future research for reform to consider the rights and entitlements of the remaining 5% of the carers to obtain the full picture and better consider the challenges faced by Australian families. Regardless of whether a separate 'Maternity Leave Act' is legislated in the near future or whether the aforementioned addition to the maternity leave provision in the *Paid Parental Leave Act 2010* is introduced, this monograph argues that the amended period of paid parental and paid maternity leave should be extended to 26 weeks each, affording mothers with a maximum of 52 weeks of paid leave to foster the mother's bond with their children and bridge the workforce gender equality gap.

CONCLUSIONS

This study critically examined the current legal landscape of paid parental leave in Australia and compared it with equivalent provisions in other OECD member countries with a nominal GDP similar to Australia's, namely, Canada, Germany and Sweden. In comparing the legal entitlements of women against the OECD member countries, major discrepancies concerning leave duration and operation were established. This research has analysed the international treaties that have informed parental leave policies, the CEDAW, ICESCR, CRC and the ILO's Conventions and Recommendations. It has explored three variants of feminism, which were applied to analyse current Australian paid parental leave provisions. This analysis led to an observation that paid parental leave provisions are categorical to cultural feminism, whereas unpaid parental leave provisions fall under liberal feminism. These observations appear inconsistent with the parental leave policies of the identified OECD member countries, whose provisions fall under the cultural and reconstructive feminist paragons, championing women's rights as mothers and, equally, as breadwinners for the family.

Further, this monograph has relied on a breadth of social and political research into how Australian paid parental leave laws have developed from their inception to the current period. These social and political findings have effectively demonstrated that not only is Australia lagging in terms of duration and generosity of parental leave, as compared with OECD equivalents, but it has also been stagnant in terms of domestic development, with Australian paid parental leave not introduced until 2010. Employer-paid parental leave was also examined, revealing that, in practice, parental leave payments are viewed as welfare payments instead of a human right, as stipulated by international treaties.

While Australia's statutory paid parental leave aims to address gender inequality, promote women's workforce participation and promote child and maternal health, the 18-week duration falls considerably short compared with other OECD member countries and fails to meet the WHO's 26-week minimum leave duration for optimal child and maternal health. On average, mothers in Canada, Germany and Sweden have up to 74 weeks of statutory paid parental leave, paid at approximately AUD700 per week following childbirth or adoption. Meanwhile, Australian mothers are only entitled to up to 18 weeks[1] of statutory paid leave weeks (less than 25% of the average entitlements of Canada, Germany and Sweden) at AUD754 per week.

Two key recommendations were made: first, an extension of Australia's current paid parental leave to total of 52 weeks for optimal child and maternal health, and second, the introduction of an individual 15-week 'maternity leave' provision exclusive to mothers, bringing the overall duration of leave available to mothers to 52 weeks, approximately 70% of the provisions offered by the featured OECD countries. These reforms might be introduced in stages. With the first recommendation to meet the 26-week recommendation of the WHO for optimal child and maternal health so that Australia can consistently meet its 'child's best interests' obligations under the CRC. This recommendation was informed by the results of the comparison with other OECD countries and considered the development of paid parental leave policies in these countries, which have shown substantial progressive increments in duration since inception. The second recommendation was made to increase the number of women returning to work instead of exiting the workforce following childbirth or adoption. The recommendations, if enacted, will advocate on Australian mothers' rights through a reconstructive feminist lens by celebrating women's differences with men (provided by the paid maternity leave) and removing any disadvantage women may have in meeting masculinised social norms (provided by paid parental leave available to both mothers and fathers at a reasonable duration). Germany's parental leave scheme was discussed as a point of reference for Australia because of Germany's similar funding of paid parental leave through general taxation and its clear and succinct legislation regarding paid parental leave rights.

The current landscape for maternal and parental leave in Australia is a long way to reaching even half of what similar OECD countries bestow mothers within their states. Is caring for children an undervalued asset in Australia? It appears otherwise, with the Morrison government's recent announcement on an additional $1.7 billion investment in childcare as part of the 2021–2022 Budget.[2] Australian Treasurer Josh Frydenberg noted that the investment,

---

1   20 weeks were announced under Federal budget of 2022, with implementation from 1 July 2022.
2   Department of Education, Skills and Employment, 'Budget 2021–22: Portfolio Budget Statements 2021–22 Budget Related Monograph No. 1.4' (Department of Education, Skills and Employment, 5 May 2021) 11 <https://www.dese.gov.au/download/11359/2021-22-portfolio-budget-statements/21785/portfolio-budget-statements-2021-22-education-skills-and-employment-portfolio/pdf>.

inter alia, 'makes child care more affordable, increases workforce participation and boosts the Australian economy by up to $1.5 billion per year'.[3] Minister for Women Marise Payne noted that 'increasing the Child Care Subsidy is an important measure that will help reduce the disincentives for women to participate in the workforce to the full extent they choose'.[4] However, Minister Payne did not address the 'difficulties experienced by employees attempting to access their organisation's work-life balance provisions, including refusal of parental leave applications.'[5] While the government's improved funding of childcare will help mothers to return to work, it does little to alter the fact that the government's parental leave scheme places the onus for the care of the newborn or newly adopted child entirely on the mother, by failing to also provide paid parental leave for fathers. While the increased funding for childcare may help mothers return to work after the 18-week paid parental leave is over, such a policy does not address the importance of raising the child at home with a parent for at least the first year of the child's life. Research suggests that parents taking paid parental leave may have had greater opportunities to implement coping strategies that assist in avoiding the occurrence of work-family conflict after re-entering the workforce.[6] 'Developing greater work–life balance and better quality of life' became an important social and economic imperative.[7]

The support of parents is instrumental in countries with the ageing population and Australia is one of such country. If the current paid parental leave landscape is not reformed, it is inevitable to ask – who cares about the next generation in Australia?

---

3 Josh Frydenberg et al, 'Making Child Care More Affordable and Boosting Workforce Participation', *The Hon Josh Frydenberg MP Treasurer of the Commonwealth of Australia* (Web Page, 5 February 2021) <https://ministers.treasury.gov.au/ministers/josh-frydenberg-2018/media-releases/making-child-care-more-affordable-and-boosting>.

4 Ibid.

5 Brough, O'Driscoll and Biggs (n 4).

6 Tammy D Allen et al, 'The Link between National Paid Leave Policy and Work-Family Conflict among Married Working Parents' (2014) 63(1) *Applied Psychology: An International Review* 5.

7 Paula Brough and Michael P O'Driscoll, 'Integrating Work and Personal Life' in *Flourishing in Life, Work and Careers: Individual Wellbeing and Career Experiences* (Edward Elgar Publishing, 2015) 377.

Printed in Australia
Ingram Content Group Australia Pty Ltd
AUHW021831270923
384297AU00001B/2